your guide to group experience

YOUR GUIDE TO GROUP EXPERIENCE

SAMUEL SOUTHARD

ABINGDON PRESS

Nashville New York

Library of Congress Cataloging in Publication Data

SOUTHARD, SAMUEL.
Your guide to group experience.

1. Group relations training. I. Title.
HM134.S66 301.18′5 73-22431

ISBN 0-687-46901-5

The material in chapter one appeared in *Religion in Life*, Summer, 1973.

Text on page 142 is from Peanuts by Charles M. Schulz © 1973 United Feature Syndicate, Inc.

The student's prayer on pages 88-90 is from the January, 1965, issue of *Journal of Religion and Health.*

MANUFACTURED BY THE PARTHENON PRESS AT
NASHVILLE, TENNESSEE, UNITED STATES OF AMERICA

contents

introduction
do i need comfort or cure?

What would you expect out of one of the group experiences that are now advertised in the newspapers, required for professional training, encouraged for managers, or promoted by churches and colleges? The array of programs will range from very controlled meetings for religious purposes to spontaneous expressions of love and hate through tears, screams, or embraces. There are so many kinds of "encounters" that you will need some guide to the one that is best for you—if you need one at all.

Are you looking for some radical change in yourself? Don't look for an answer through the newspaper advertisements on the "human potential movement." The best research on small groups, by Lieberman, Yalom, and Miles, give a clear warning against group surgery that would produce a new man. The danger is especially great when a leader and a participant both think that magical lasting changes will come out of a weekend "marathon" or brief sensitivity training.

In *Encounter Groups: First Facts,* Dr. Lieberman and his associates do find groups which provide useful opportunities for human beings to explore and express themselves with others. A group can teach us how to know when others care for us and how to receive that care. But an encounter group is not a cure for deep-seated emotional problems.

This evidence from a study of seventeen different types of groups might seem contradictory to the glowing accounts on encounters that you have received from a friend. The friend may have told of the intense interaction and great surge of feeling that came through a weekend retreat. Certainly it is true that strangers can assemble for a session and interact intensely, but they then become strangers again. The relationships are deep, but temporary. We need and want these experiences, for we learn something about ourselves from them. But these are not the experiences that alter people permanently.

Salvation and Healing

Suppose your need is for cure rather than care? The need may be for some radical shift in your loyalties or reevaluation of your purpose in living. If so, your need is for a type of group experience that is much older than the modern encounter group.

The depth approach to personal problems through groups has its roots in American religion and medicine. The first approach to radical change was made by the Reverend Jonathan Edwards in the 1740s. He called for a public awareness that a person did not know himself and therefore could not know God. He said that people were talking about love, forgiveness, and repentance with no clear awareness of the impact which those words should have in a person's life. The religious words of the day had no meaning because the mind and the emotion of the people were separated. Jonathan Edwards developed revival techniques that brought emotions to the surface where they could be described, socialized, explained. "Inquirers" came to the home of Mr. Edwards on Mondays and Tuesdays to sit as a group and talk about their awareness of a greater power which would direct and give meaning to their lives. Although the pastor spent some time in private conversations with individuals, most of his work was through public exhortations in the church and group meetings with those who sought to be awakened as they talked before others in his home. Each person described the stirring of his heart. The pastor offered interpretation, guidance, and assurance.

The Methodist class meeting followed much of the same methodology in the early nineteenth century on the old southwest frontier. On most occasions, members of the society met weekly to testify before others of their victories or failures. Each person was edified by the testimony of others and educated by the leader and others concerning his own experience. A modification of the class meeting came when the group would sing hymns as the leader went quietly from one member to another and heard their individual testimonies of experiences. In the early days of the "great awakening," inquiry groups might meet for six months so that evangelists and class leaders would know that a real change had taken place in the life of a convert before admission to church membership. After admission, the individual continued in a class meeting for purposes of stabilizing his experience and continuing his education in the Christian faith.

The in-depth experience of the Methodist revival and the intimate sharing of the class meeting could not survive the growing sophistication of Methodists and others in the last half of the nineteenth century. The class meeting grew less personal and finally was abandoned in the twentieth century. But for almost one hundred years, the revival and the class meeting were major attempts to promote a radical shift in loyalty and a stable growth toward new expectation for the self in relation to God and man.

A second attempt to provide long term cure for major distress came from a group that was almost untouched by the revivalism of the nineteenth century. In the early 1900s, the Reverend Elwood Worcester combined religion and medicine in a clinic at the Emmanuel Episcopal Church in Boston. He and prominent physicians began meetings for tubercular patients who needed understanding and courage to endure chronic disease. Soon the demand came for sessions with people who complained of a wide range of illnesses, most of which we would call psychosomatic. All persons in the classes would receive physical examination and any necessary medical care. But the main emphasis of the program was upon religious resources for the crises of life. The Reverend Worcester gave this subtitle to *Religion and Medicine:* "The Moral Control of Nervous Disorders."

The senior physician in the Emmanuel Church clinic was Dr. Joseph H. Pratt. He became known as the father of group therapy. The movement gained a new technique in the 1920s through the introduction of psychodrama by Dr. Moreno. Mental patients dramatized before others the typical scenes of their childhood or marriage. Long-buried emotions surfaced for recognition by the patient and interpretation by his fellows.

World War II accelerated the need for group work, for

there were more psychiatric casualties than trained workers. Individual consultation was still available in some cases, but more and more meetings were held for a dozen patients at a time. That which began as necessity soon proved to be a positive benefit. There was mutual support and socializing. Men found strength in the group itself.

"Group therapy" became a term for medical treatment which would relieve psychic suffering through membership in a controlled group. A highly trained person would serve as leader and helper toward healing. The assumption of therapy was that people were in deep trouble and needed controlled and continuous help for healing. In some cases the healing would be a radical reevaluation of the self and a movement toward new purposes in life. In other cases it might be reeducation for more adequate adjustment in living. Whatever the goals, caring was a part of curing, but the basic assumption was that people needed something more than a brief social encounter.

Education for Living

The original program of Worcester and Pratt was a combination of education and medical treatment. Group therapy emphasized the medical model. The other facet, education, was given a renewed impetus in 1946 when the executive director of the Connecticut Fair Employment Practices Act asked Dr. Kurt Lewin to help train leaders who could reduce group tensions. The research that grew out of the early training laboratory was "electrifying" to the staff. They found that both staff members and students could benefit from direct confrontation of opinions in an objective manner. Each person could observe his own reactions and be helped by comments from the group. The interpersonal style of each student and staff member became clear. The meetings ended with greater understanding of group behavior.

The National Training Laboratory grew out of this "T-group" (training group). The tradition is education. Instead of involuntary patients, the members are voluntary teachers or businessmen. The emphasis is upon increasing effectiveness at work rather than on curing an illness or patient with chronic disease. The leader is a teacher who presents himself as an equal rather than as the specialist in a medical or psychological field. In the May, 1967, issue of *The New Yorker*, the Director of the National Laboratories, Leland Bradford, wrote that group therapy is not conducted in T-groups. Instead, the emphasis is on group *dynamics:* that is, learning about self and others in interpersonal relations. But the groups are not intended as a substitute for psychotherapy.

The T-groups became popular in management circles. The Harvard Business School developed a case history approach to management decisions, and the Massachusetts Institute of Technology established a research center for group dynamics. Top executives met for two-week workshops on "back-home" problems. They became more aware of the human element in management decisions and their own style of managing people.

The National Education Association began to use a variation of T-groups in the 1960s. Powerful forces for change were moving in schools through student protests and civil rights. Bitter tension and physical violence had to be met. How could contrary groups be reconciled?

"Sensitivity groups" were promoted as one answer to

group tension. Teachers and administrators were trained to "unfreeze" participants, establish contact between people, self-disclosure, manage confrontation, increase objectivity in observation of self and others. There was a constant alternation between "there and then" material and "here and now." That is, discussions might begin with a problem area in the home school district, but soon moved to observations about the way in which this member was relating now to the group. Could he relate his present feelings among these people to his style of management or teaching back home?

The educational process might begin with the simulation of a situation back home. One member of the group might play the part of a beleaguered teacher. Another member would be a militant black student or ghetto spokesman. As the play progressed, participants would be asked for their impressions: "How do you feel right now?" Others would offer comments, feedback phrases that had eluded the participant's awareness: "Did you know that you said so and so?"

The general objective of education in sensitivity is to be fully aware of yourself and participate in a group, and yet know what you are doing and understand what is happening in the meeting. The head and the heart are to know each other.

The Questionable Encounter

The established groups for therapy and education are now being threatened by groups that exalt experience and reject "intellectualizations." The emphasis of the new encounter groups is upon "sensory awareness," which is to be achieved by a variety of body contacts and bold denunciations of others in the group. Feelings are exploited in marathon sessions of twenty-four or forty-eight hours. Each person is to have an "experience," whether he has time to assimilate it or not.

The encounter groups share many of the excesses of nineteenth-century revivals. In that day, "heart religion" was lifted up and "head religion" was despised. An orgy of emotion characterized many religious meetings. Bodily exercises, including "jerks" and "treeing the devil," were common. Mature ministers could promote a union of head and heart without wild displays, but unwise or overzealous preachers worked their audiences into states of hysteria. Mass evangelism was branded by the uncontrolled results of some meetings.

The same condemnation is coming upon modern exponents of emotion for its own sake. With a crash-program mentality, the good results to T-groups and group therapy are pushed to absurd extremes. Self-disclosure can be prolonged until it is psychoanalysis without controls. The person is ripped apart, and no one has time to get him together again. The value of involvement is exploited into a weekend of continuous insistence that everyone tell something that is intimate, and usually hostile. The need for bodily expression and a friendly embrace is carried beyond the boundaries of discretion into hitting, touching, feeling, kissing, and sexual intercourse (this is a paraphrase of Dr. Irvin Yalom's critique of new groups, in his *Theory and Practice of Group Psychotherapy* [New York Basic Books, 1970], pp. 355-56). The desperate need for authenticity and intimacy in modern American culture has caused a mushroom growth of "human potential" workshops. Dr. Irvin Yalom counted two hundred encounter and related groups in the Palo Alto area of California, population one hundred thousand. Esalen, at Big Sur, California, has over fifty thousand in various programs held throughout the country. Newspapers carry advertisements for encounter groups, psychodrama, self-actualization, mind-body connections, gestalt, yoga, zen, grope groups. These are open to almost anyone for fees ranging from one dollar to fifteen dollars a session.

Controlling the Encounter

Despite excesses, encounter and other human potential groups are being recommended to churches, executive groups, school systems. How can we evaluate the need for such a program, examine the credentials of those who lead, and control the results?

First, do you really want a training session or encounter group? If you know that a changing neighborhood demands better understanding on the part of all people, then a confrontation group may be very helpful. Or if a group of young people in the church are looking for a retreat in which the meaning of faith will come more alive, they may benefit from religiously oriented sensitivity training. If there has just been a change in the chief executives of a denomination, several of these may go with other leaders to a workshop on human relations.

But the problems of your church or organization may not be met by a group of people talking for a weekend. As a school trustee, you may find that morale is low because decision-making is handled in an authoritarian fashion. This is the impediment to communication. People are scared to tell the superintendent what they know is going on. He always takes criticism personally. If you brought principals and superintendents into an encounter group, there would certainly be some feelings expressed. But would the results justify the explosion and resentment? Should poor management be handled by a group of subordinates, or by the school board?

Again, you may find employee morale low and absenteeism rampant. Employees may tell you that better communication between the workers will be important *after* you have raised the pay and improved the working conditions.

A training laboratory at the wrong time or with a vulnerable participant will do more harm than good. In one mental health center, the director asked for staff development workshops, but attended infrequently. Staff members voiced their dissatisfaction with his leadership. He was a good therapist but a poor administrator. The director was unsure of his position anyway. He had hoped that the workshop would make people more sympathetic, easier to work with. Instead, he had to face open opposition that was zeroed in on his most conspicuous weakness—which he would not change.

In contrast, the staff of a large downtown church invited a trainer to lead them in a weekend retreat after the trainer had been with various groups in the church during the week. The trainer summarized for the staff his findings from the week. Some of his remarks caused the pastor to ask if he had shown enough confidence in one of the assistant pastors. The assistant pastor did not think so. The two men clarified their own feelings about each other, and other staff members fed back their impressions of the relationship of these men to each other, and to the rest of the staff. "Well," said the pastor, "I guess that we would never have cleared this up without some specific focus—and leisure—for this discussion. Thanks."

A second consideration is the *type* of workshop you desire. The church staff wanted an educational experience. They were not in need of therapy. Similarly, many church couples groups want an enriching and growing group. Suggestions for better relationships are welcomed. They are healthy people with resources to use intelligently and accurately. They readily pick up ideas from each other and use them responsibly.

But if many of the participants are chronically neurotic, the purpose will need to be more therapeutic. Their patterns of living must be untangled and new resources added to their living before they can be restored to health. More time, stricter controls, and specialized leadership will be necessary.

Any of the following groups are helpful *if* you plan ahead and announce the aims for which each is designed:

Enrichment: a series of seminars or a weekend for healthy people who concentrate on a specific such as family interaction, morals and marriage, teen-agers and parents, faith and doubt, drugs and dependency, loneliness and companionship. The meeting may be open to any person in your church or organization who seems to have an appropriate interest in the subject, and it may be led by persons with a variety of background and training.

Encounter: sessions in which people from varying social or ethnic groups openly state their prejudices about each other and learn how it feels to walk in another's shoes.

Participants should be chosen for their representative function or leadership for potential reconciliation.

Establishment: managerial or professional persons meet for growth of interpersonal skills which will aid their competence in work. If the people are going to be in the same plant or hospital for the next ten years, they must focus more upon common problems in the job and less upon self-revelations of past history and present prejudices. If they will be scattered after the meeting, the admission of gut-reactions may be more frequent, but there will have to be some covenant about sharing secrets. The leader for these groups is often a person from the profession or business who has had specialized training in leadership development.

Examination: therapy for disturbed people, preceded by psychological consultation and led by a psychiatrist, clinical psychologist, social worker, nurse, or chaplain with graduate training in psychotherapy. The purpose is to examine the complexities of sick thinking and distorted relationships in a fellowship of concerned people under skilled leadership.

After a decision on the type of group you will sponsor, turn to a third issue, the qualifications of persons who will lead the workshop. Look for help from the National Training Laboratories, the American Group Psychotherapy Association, the adult education section of the National Education Association. Any of these organizations may be contacted through your county or state community mental center, school superintendent, community college, or state university. Several Protestant denominations maintain a staff that recommends personnel or conducts enrichment, encounter, and establishment seminars.

A fourth question is personal: what will you gain from sponsoring or attending these sessions? If you wish to know yourself better, to gain more understanding of those with whom you will work, then the first three types of seminars will be appropriate. If, on the other hand, you are really worried about yourself, seek some professional guidance on the type of group which you should enter. Psychotherapy may be recommended, either individually or in a group. Or you may find that your fears are unfounded. You're not sick, just lonely and confused. The shocks of life are showing, and you need some reassessment through a caring fellowship organized for renewal. It is this type of enrichment, the renewal group, that has become very popular in churches.

Some Preliminary Questions

When we get to the question of personal gain from a group experience, there are more specific questions that should be raised.

The first one is: "Do you seek this on a voluntary basis?" This question has received increasing prominence as more and more psychiatrists and others have treated persons who became psychotic during a marathon or new group experience. Dr. Joel Steinberg, of Case-Western Reserve University, has noted that psychiatric casualties in groups are usually the people who were persuaded to attend by their spouses or sent by their church or business. If a person is being persuaded to attend the group experience, he would do well to see a counselor before the experience to weigh his choices. He may need group therapy rather than sensitivity training, or he may be in greater need of individual counsel.

A second question is: "What do you plan to contribute to or get out of this particular experience?" A practical businessman may say that some of his friends attended a training lab and thought that it improved their awareness of employee relationships. We would hope that this man could be directed toward a training lab rather than toward a marathon sensitivity group in which people are encouraged to give gut reactions and regress to a primitive state of being. One executive went to the latter type of meeting and returned with disgust for any type of emotional expression. He said: "I don't care to be like that doctor who confessed all of his conflicts with his wife and finally lay on the floor, curled up and sucking his thumb like a two-year-old. But the leader thought it was great and really got him into that position."

On the other hand, a person who speaks of deep conflicts or serious difficulties would certainly be referred to group therapy under a professional person who could evaluate the risk of this individual participation and control his treatment.

Third: "Would you be willing to ask a professional counselor if his group experience is the best thing for you at the present time?" He should be able to evaluate your need for cure or care, for radical self-surgery versus social experience. When your needs and expectations have been clarified, you will find less danger and more satisfaction in the group that he recommends. In some instances he will not recommend any type of group. The one session with him or her or a series of individual conferences may be the kind of help that you need.

Fourth: "Do you know what kind of behavior and rules are expected in these group sessions?" You may fantasize a group experience like those publicized from California which include group hugging without swimming suits in a pool. Or you may think that you will sit among dignified businessmen in an executive suite and discuss the best way to manage people for profit.

Fifth: "Who is the leader of this group?" You may not know this and may need to ask some professional therapist or some people who have been in the group that have interested you. They should be able to describe the leader according to the four categories that were developed by Dr. Irvin Yalom and Dr. Morton Lieberman in "A Study of Encounter Group Casualties," which was a chapter of progress in *Group and Family Therapy*, edited by Clifford Fagger and Helen Caplan.

Four types of leader behaviors were distinguished by Lieberman and Yalom. The first was a charismatic leader who continually sought to stimulate the group through his interaction with them. At times he may threaten an individual so much that persons withdraw from the group, or he may lead a person to say so much that the individual is embarrassed to continue in the group or begins to lose social and psychological control of himself. The result is a psychiatric casualty which is a higher risk under this type of leadership than any of the others.

A second type of leader will emphasize caring. He shows concern for every comment and is obviously supportive of each person in the group. Under this type of leadership, a group may not move very far, but it will be secure.

A third type of leader will seek to give meaning to statements made by participants or behaviors that are observed in the group. He attributes significance to the words and actions of persons in a way that increases self-understanding without loss of face. He is a wise teacher who can put into words the vague feelings of an individual or summarize and make sense out of a series of confused actions. This teaching group is most successful and shows highest rate of personal growth.

A fourth type of leader is a manager. He steers the group as a whole rather than working with individual or interpersonal relations. Rarely is there any confrontation or challenge to individuals.

You may wonder at the lack of emphasis upon a particular school of thought in these categories. The researchers found that ideology had no significant relationship to success in therapy. The major variable is his manner of relating to participants in the group.

How are you going to relate to participants in the group? This is the question that will come up again and again in any interpersonal encounter. The rest of this book will introduce you to the questions that participants raise as they move through a group experience.

The emphasis upon "sharing" will usually prompt the first question of a new member. Why do all these people insist that I talk about myself? Why can't I just sit and listen?

About the same time, another question pops up: "What kind of people am I with?" We become very self-conscious and conscious of others who are asked to talk about themselves. We wonder if we can trust ourselves to say the right thing and trust these other people to understand and hold our confidences.

As seminars progress, we hear much talk about the "group experience." Just what is it? Or we may have heard others speak about their experience and try to figure out why it had to be with other people. What's so special about sharing in a circle or something like that?

Another early question is the icebreaker: "How do we begin?" We may have heard of people who sat for many hours in silence, while others tell us of first sessions in which the most intimate revelations are made. Just how does all that get started?

These are the beginning questions, which we discuss in chapters 1 through 4.

Then there are some thoughtful questions that emerge as we meet more often. Will I be able to really say what I want to? Should I tell some of the events that are painful, reveal some of the memories that put me down? This is the question of personal failure. Those who can speak of their embarrassing moments, and receive interpretation and support, are usually the ones who say they received acceptance and understanding in this group work.

But some people are very worried about self-control when they speak of painful or disgraceful experiences. Or they just naturally cry whenever they reveal tender emotion. As we watch people around us, we usually ask, how about me? Can I make disclosures with composure?

These are the middle-range questions of an on-going group, which we discuss in chapters 5 and 6.

As we move toward the closing phases of this relationship, some people begin to make decisions and announce changes that they will work for from here on. Naturally this raises the questions, have they made a good decision, and could I do the same? These are especially vexing questions for the Charlie Browns who are so indecisive. For them to make any decisions will be a great victory.

Some folks become preoccupied with making any decisions—just one. Others are able to make up their minds—they needed the group to make them sensitive to their own inner longings and to the needs of others so that their decisions could be more realistic.

When we come toward the last sessions, or hours, there is a problem of group support. Are we going to continue to find this kind of understanding in some other group? Do we need it? Should we modify our demands?

Most of us continue to need someone to lean on, whether it be in the family, church, fraternity, or convalescent after-care clinic. People may resent the idea of continuing dependency until they realize that all of us must look to others for support at specific times in our lives, and some people have been deprived of so much support in childhood that they need long-term support as they face adult responsibility. The answer to dependency is that some of us just need a group now and then to check out our understanding of things, some need periodic help when things don't go right, and a few must drop into some kind of substitute family at least once a month for years to come—whether it be Alcoholics Anonymous or a weekly Sunday school class. Everybody needs somebody sometimes, and the modern group experience is one way to meet some of those normal needs for affiliation. So let's begin.

chapter 1
why talk about me?

In a group, input determines output. You get out as much for yourself as you are willing to put yourself into the experience. *You* are the ingredient that makes the group grow. But you may question this assumption of the "human potential" movement.

Why this emphasis upon shared feelings? Can't I have opinions for myself without telling everyone in this meeting? Two or three will do all the talking, so why exert myself to get in the conversation? I can learn by listening.

If you accept the silent attitude, you may be a drifter instead of a learner. How will you or anyone else know that you have grown through this group unless you show and tell? If others take risks or try to help, what does this say about you on the sideline?

Drifting with the crowd is an easy out in modern society. You can make a comfortable living as a "yes sayer." If so, your mission in life will be to sense the thinking of powerful people in your office or society and conform to their wishes. Whenever possible you seek to please people and make circumstances easy.

You may not like to be called a "nice guy" all the time, but the label may be accurate. What have you done to show personal convictions? In what ways are you an individual apart from crowd approval?

You may retreat grandly from these biting questions and say: "Well, I know myself, and that is enough." If you say this, you must confront a second problem of silence, which is hypocrisy. Do you really know yourself or are you deceived?

Young adults are quite sensitive about concealment. Why? Because a previous generation was so blind to faults. Our nineteenth-century forebears made resolutions on the basis of high ideals and did not commit themselves to think less than the culture demanded. Negative thoughts were repressed. Uncomfortable feelings were denied. People did not say how they really felt. There was no admission of the unconscious urges, anxieties, fears, and instinctual forces that drive us. These denials made hypocrisy a major moral problem and hysteria a prevalent medical diagnosis.

The inner warfare of the self-deceived has many symptoms: cynicism, fault-finding, intolerance, punctiliousness, restlessness, self-importance, bitterness, anxiety, self-pity. We do not see ourselves as others see us, and we often are not sure of the way we see ourselves. Instead of an open admission of confusion, we may retreat into the projection of blame or inaccurate accusations against self.

There is a special problem of hypocrisy among young adults. This is the flight-into-life syndrome. You pursue one worthy ambition with all your talent and pull the rest of yourself out of line. When desire rises up to dominate all the rest because you are young and attractive, this may seem good at the time to you and others. But it is impulsive adaptation to the moment. You are really satisfying some desires of which you are vaguely aware and over which you have little control.

A young husband fled from love into financial and social security. Soon after marriage he bought a boat and spent all day Sunday on the water. When his wife protested that she did not want to sail every Sunday and would like to attend church from time to time, he said that the boat built up his sense of command. It gave him the necessary strength to compete with other junior executives during the week.

In the evenings the husband pored over market reports and made notes for calls on the stock market. When his wife said that she would like to move out of the apartment and into a home, he said that they must first build up enough income to live on the interest. After they had accumulated a hundred thousand dollars he would buy a house.

The husband stayed up so late at night that the wife usually fell asleep alone. After several months of this she asked why he never made love to her. He replied: "You said when we were first married that you wanted to have a child as soon as possible. We must wait until we have a house before we can have a child; besides, I am tired in the evenings and really would not be able to satisfy you."

When the wife finally persuaded her husband to see a marriage counselor with her, the husband spent three interviews in self-justification. He had all the right reasons for pursuing worthy activities. But he missed a very personal one: he was afraid he would fail if he tried to be tender. In part this was a problem of sexual impotence. But it was more complicated. The man thought that he was incapable of satisfying the intimate needs of another person in any way. His family had always put him down and rejected him. Why should he expose himself to ridicule now from one whom he desired? By fleeing into activity he escaped from the possibility of hurting himself and disappointing his wife.

Stages in Self-Understanding

Both drifting and deceit can be mastered by confrontation and confession. We can know ourselves if we can take the risk of sharing our opinions and feelings. When we test our assumptions and decisions against others in a group, we are more likely to learn reality. Other people may not accept our fantasy about ourselves and our projections of assumptions upon others.

What happens to us as we move through the group process toward self-understanding?

Discovery of the self usually begins in collapse of an idol. The sham-self cannot survive open disclosure. A young lady met this truth when she was arguing with some men in her group. One of the girls observed that this young lady was quite competitive with men. When asked why, she said: "Why she never pays any attention when one of us girls is speaking, but she jumps right in whenever one of the men takes a strong stand. Then she seems to delight in taking on one man after another in the group."

The young lady in question was amazed at this opinion. She protested: "I have always been feminine. My place is with the girls. I think that charm and poise are better than pushiness."

One of the men asked why the young lady always pushed in on the conversation when men dominated the conversation.

She replied: "Well, I learned early in life that a girl has to speak up if she is going to be heard. I had three brothers. They would have run all over me if I had not said what I thought. If you are going to get ahead in life, you have to state your opinions and stand by them."

The group then discussed the obvious. The young lady was relating to men as she had to her aggressive brothers. She had never thought of this as unusual behavior. Now she began to see that not all men were like her brothers, and that some women had other ways of being heard.

No idol falls lightly. Concerted effort is needed to topple a pseudo-self. This is why group discussions are often superior to individual counseling among normal people. We can work together in dislodging an illusion. A person who is deceived by himself may not respond to the observations of one person, but when he hears the same opinion from a dozen different individuals, he begins to think that there is some logic in their conclusions. Perhaps he should reconsider himself.

A journey into the self is a second stage in self-awareness. Healthy people may do much of this useful work outside a group setting. This is why a retreat often offers periods of silence or free time between group discussions. It is in these moments of meditation that we can reexamine the state of our soul. Just what kind of person are we?

Some of our thoughts may be provoked by what others have said to us or by what we have identified with in the struggles of another in the group. By remembering what was said, we take others on our journey. Also, we can stop along the way to check the reality of our perceptions. At the next group meeting we may indicate what we have learned and how it stirred our thinking.

Why go back to tell anybody? The answer is twofold: we may think too much or too little. Thinking too much is an obsessive trait. You may spin off many wild fantasies from some incidental remark in the last meeting. You may have decided that all were against you because your remarks were interrupted by others, or no one paid attention to your first attempts to talk. You then went out into the fields and felt sorry for yourself: "That's the way it always is. No one ever listens to me. I know that I am no good. Why did I come to this meeting anyway?"

It is so easy to misperceive. A shy young man spoke up in the third meeting of his group. He mildly disagreed with the dominate person at that time. He was completely silent for the next two meetings. When the group leader asked him about this during an individual interview, the young man said: "I should not have lost my temper. I know that everyone was embarrassed because of the way that I yelled at that conceited prude. I must learn to control myself better."

The leader expressed amazement in this self-perception: "Why I could hardly hear what you said in the group. Who told you that you were yelling at anybody? I thought that your remarks were well-balanced and accurate. Why did you decide that they were inappropriate?"

The young man said that he had always been afraid of losing his temper. He thought that any disagreement was a sign of belligerence. Perhaps he had overestimated his volume and his vehemence.

Some people overestimate what they have done in the group and others underestimate. You may have thought that you made no contribution and felt silly after the meeting. But then someone will remark at dinner that he had been thinking about your words ever since the afternoon session. You did not realize the importance of your few thoughts.

Saying too little may mean a low evaluation of our contribution, or it may be a lack of courage in continuing the self-disclosure. Of course, the two sides are related. We may shut up just at the time that others turn to us and show interest. That's why we become quiet—too much interest has been shown. Despite the discomfort, we need to continue the inner exploration. It may be through more conversation, through the group, or through more dialogue with the self in secret. Both are probably necessary.

If you are faithful in this, you will probably find some block in your thinking. You just cannot think through a painful or bewildering subject. When you're stuck, someone else may get you on to a new track of thought.

A twenty-five-year-old man, George Horn, told his group: "I have never realized how much I needed brothers and sisters, people like you. I grew up with my uncle and aunt, who were kind to me, but they gave most of their attention and all of their affection to their own children. I just stood around and watched. This is the first time that people my own age have really been interested in what is going on inside of me."

The next day, George sat silently in the group for half an hour. When someone asked why he looked so puzzled, he said: "I can't figure something out. I now realize that a group like this is very important to me. I also realized something that I didn't say yesterday, which is that my wife means all the world to me. She really cares for me, and I'm so happy with our son. But in the midst of all this happiness, I get depressed."

A member of the group asked him if this were a constant thing or an occasional reaction.

"Well," said George, "I guess it just happens at certain times—but they are the times when I should be most happy! Like at Christmas my wife and I decorated the tree; it was the first one that I had ever helped decorate, and we had a grand time watching our son play with his toys. But while he was taking his nap, I sat in my chair and almost cried. I just felt so sad, and I did not know why. It doesn't make sense."

"Oh yes it does!" said a friend beside him. "You told us yesterday that no one paid attention to you when you were young, and you just said that this was the first year that you had ever decorated a Christmas tree. Think of the contrast between what you are doing with your son and what was not done with you as a little fellow. That is enough to make anybody depressed."

"Sure," said a middle-aged woman. "And you may get angry, too, like I do. No one ever paid much attention to me at holidays or gave me many gifts. I can't stand to hear my husband tell about the happy things he did as a child at Christmas. It's unfair, because he is telling it to share himself with the children. But it just goes all over me. I think he is bragging about something that I was denied."

George frowned. "I guess what you tell me is true, but I don't like it. I want to be happy when my family is happy." The group leader said: "Your family will be giving you good things, and you will be giving good things to them. But they cannot completely fill up the hunger from the past. They can only feed you in the present. Your memory will pull you down once in a while, but the love of your life together now will pull you back up. Just watch those holidays."

The young man was moving toward a third stage in self-awareness in which we become conscious of painful memories and disguised urges, find a place for them in our lives, and find a place for ourselves in the family, society, and world. This acceptance of self and dedication to serve may come gradually or as a sudden illumination. A marathon group will push for instantaneous insight. All the lights are supposed to go on at one time. But you may be "turned on" for only twenty-four hours. When you get back home, you cannot maintain the same glow. The realities of daily compromises may be too much. Or, you may have said more than you can assimilate. You are not yet aware of all the connections and ramifications of your new decisions. A powerful thought pulls a lot of current. It may take you some time to trace down the old "wiring" of your relationships and look for possible shortages and frayed endings. Stronger relationships may need to be built before you can realize all that you have talked about. You may need to be rewired for 220 voltage to sustain a new light. "Rewiring" is one way of saying that we must re-examine our inner thoughts and our relationships to others. We will spend some time in tracing the roots of our inner thoughts so that the major attitudes of our life are consistent with each other. For example, in a later chapter we will consider the story of a young man who preached the love of God and loyalty to his friends. But he found through a group experience that he had neglected his wife. He had never made the connection between what he professed and what he practiced in his own home.

Knowledge Is Not Enough

The purpose of self-awareness is stronger service. A person who knows himself can make a realistic dedication to life. He is thinking of the contribution that he can make to others rather than the contribution that they can make to him.

You may not catch this purpose in the first meeting of your group. There will be so much emphasis upon self-declaration that you may think we are being trained in selfishness. Why are these people so preoccupied with their own thoughts and feelings?

What is selfishness? David Riesman, in his book *Individualism Reconsidered,* stated that the selfish person has no real self and no fondness for the self. He must continually seek security in terms of conquest and power to compensate for his lack of self-love. He is not interested in himself, but only in others' evaluations of himself. He shines in their reflected light.

We can show consistent concern for others when we first are at peace with ourselves. The happiness, growth, and freedom of our inner life will increase the capacity to share ourselves with others. The person who has a conviction of his own worth will be able to contribute something worthwhile to others. We cannot possibly give away to others what we cannot give to ourselves.

But the movement from awareness to commitment is not automatic. Some persons gain self-knowledge and are content to preen their egos forever. Like Narcissus they sit on the bank and look into the pool, enamored of their own reflection.

Ceaseless introspection is sick. We must know ourselves,

but the purpose of that knowledge goes beyond the self. There must be an act of the will to move self-love into service.

Will power begins in possibility. The group experience will teach us who we are and what we can do. We will learn that some courses of action are not appropriate because we lack the talent. An aggressive and impulsive college student told the members of a group that his ambition was to "serve the Lord" as a pastor: "I want to help people in their trouble." "What!" exclaimed another group member. "The way you push people around I don't see how you would help anybody but yourself." Another participant added: "You never listen to us here. You interrupt and demand. What would you have to offer a person in trouble?"

The student was quite surprised by this confrontation. He countered: "God will supply all of my needs; he will lead me to do the right thing. You people just don't have faith." People shook their heads and said that he was deceived. He would not hear anyone now, so how could he listen to anyone in trouble when he was a minister?

Several years later I met the former student at a business college. He explained that he had tried to be a part-time pastor when he entered divinity school, but found that the people were too stubborn and hardhearted. He had taken a promotional job in a neighboring city and was now enrolled in a course on salesmanship: "Because I really can get things done in this line of work. I get out and knock on doors—*you* might say I knock people down. But anyway, I get the message across, and it's a good living."

The young man has never heard what the group tried to

tell him. He still does not listen. Without this talent, he failed as a pastor.

The power of the will is limited both by talent and by opportunity. Our talents cannot be used unless someone needs us. They must recognize a need and also accept our confidence in service.

An American Indian stated during a student retreat that he would get a law degree and return to the reservation to fight for the rights of his people. During the weekend, other students observed the way that this man related to them and demonstrated his ability. By Sunday evening they were ready to encourage him in the continuation of his mission, for as one of them said: "You don't have a chip on your shoulder that would antagonize a white jury. Also, you speak well and will see issues clearly. Go to it."

The student was in college on the G.I. Bill of Rights. Both opportunity and talent were available to him, and the group had confirmed his will to serve.

But what do we do about people who have talent and opportunity, but make no commitment? Then we must begin to think about the will as a power in the past, present, and future.

A strong will considers the relation of the past to the present and moves toward goals for the future. The young Indian knew from his past experience the injustices of his race. He sees the present opportunity to study and prepare. The future is envisioned as a time of specific service in his chosen profession.

If the time dimensions are out of joint, commitment is imperfect. Will that concentrates on the past is paralyzed. You may have someone in your group who continually thinks about what he *should* have done. He may be filled with regrets for a number of mistakes. Or a young lady may speak angrily about her strengths and weaknesses, but take no action based upon these insights. She justifies her inaction by saying: "Since I know this about myself, there is nothing I can do. That's just the way I am." The group needs to concentrate on the present and future with her. What is she willing to experience and commit to other people right now? Does she have any hope for the future or any faith in herself? Is there any love in her for other persons that would lead toward a commitment of her talents for future service?

In therapy groups there is much concentration upon the past. Hidden desires must be unearthed. Much conversation might be necessary to dislodge these blocks in motivation. Sometimes the group will dramatize some early scene in life that destroyed a child's sense of achievement. When the painful experience is relived, a person can ask himself: "Am I still as miserable and unworthy as they thought I was then?"

Sensitivity groups concentrate more on the present. "What are you feeling in this moment of time?" There is an emphasis upon the immediate investment of a person in this group. What is he willing to share in this hour or during this weekend? If a person invests much of himself in the group discussion, then he has reliable evidence of will power for future growth.

The danger with a present orientation is fascination with our self-image and preoccupation with our own desires. This has led to a new social disease, "group addiction." Some persons move from one marathon to another, from one sensitivity lab to another. We usually recognize these people because they tell the same story over and over again. It becomes a practiced monologue with which they are fascinated.

The group may move an individual ahead by asking how his present insight will contribute to his future commitments. Or we may be in a group that is task oriented. Our purpose has already been stated, and we are to relate on the basis of a project to be undertaken or a professional skill to be developed. Confrontation groups for social change can bring present, task, and future together. As one member plays the role of a black and is abused by another member in the guise of a segregationist, each of us closely watches the emotion of the "victim." If he is too tight, or if he explodes with anger, we say that he must try again before he is ready for future service in a demonstration. If he is cool and competent, we confirm his ability to do the job. He is ready for tomorrow because of what he has demonstrated today.

Each of these tasks requires commitment and insight. We must practice self-disclosure to be sure that we see ourselves correctly. We must listen to the disclosures of others to enhance our own sensitivity to the way we are like others and the way we are different. We must tell and show to grow.

But what about the environment that best encourages personal growth? It will obviously be composed of people who sit with us in a circle or participate with us in various psychological exercises. This awareness leads to a new set of questions: What kind of people are with us in this group? They and the leader will create the climate of opinion in which an individual will flourish or wither. Are they like us in their expectations and interests? Which one will be a comfort, and which one will confront us?

chapter 2 who are these people?

With whom am I talking about myself? This is your inevitable question as people gather for their first meeting. You have decided to tell your story, but what kind of people are listening? Will your words fall upon stony ears or into wise and attentive minds? And what will you learn from the people who will be seated around a circle with you?

Sometimes we know the answers to these questions before a session begins. All of the people may have been picked for this meeting by a business. Or students that you have known in college are now with you in a sharing session for graduate students.

If you never have seen the people before, you can learn a good deal by listening to their preliminary questions. They will usually say enough for you to obtain an accurate idea of the composition of the group, the characteristics of the people and the goals they are seeking.

One of the most frequent inquiries will be: "How can I be more alive, know myself better?" If you hear this, you're probably headed toward a sensitivity group. These people around you are interested in an intense emotional impact. If they add: "I want to learn how to handle myself better and understand how to get along with people in my work," then you're in a training lab (T-group) to improve human relations skills.

The stated concerns or expectations of your associates will give you a general idea of why you're together. Awareness of yourself and others should help you do a job with people. But how are you going to get along in this group experience?

When you and others are *picked* for this experience, the initial push is coming from outside yourself. But maybe you are here because of internal pressures. You want to know: "How can I be more alive *now?*" If you hear others say the same thing, then you can look for a fast buildup toward immediate expression of beliefs and feelings. This often distinguishes the encounter group or marathon lab from the more leisurely buildup of a two-week T-group. The key word in an encounter group will probably be confrontation. Participants will be pushing for a maximum of openness and honesty. Reserve and defensiveness will soon be shorn away by vivid denunciations. Or if you can maintain your defenses for a few hours, they will be worn away by the sheer fatigue of twenty-four to forty-eight hours in a marathon.

The "now" emphasis became popular in the 1960s when militant blacks confronted teachers, police, and members of the white establishment. There was much anger around such terms as white racism, discrimination, and prejudice. Sometimes the persons who came to these groups had another question in mind: "What can we do to decrease tensions in our community?" If this question was asked many times, the group moved toward some plan for organizational change. If not, individuals either proclaimed that they felt better because feelings were openly discharged against an enemy, or people said that they now had a better understanding of the beliefs and feelings of their opponent.

Sometimes a group is asking, how they can be closer to God and their neighbors? This question usually leads to an emphasis upon Bible reading and the sharing of religious experience. Prayer and meditation are valued. People hope they will understand themselves as religious individuals, know more of God's will for their lives, and be more sensitive to his command of love for others.

You may have heard of groups in which any of these questions were asked. As you look at the people who will be with you for some kind of interpersonal dialogue you can usually say: "Well at least we are not coming together because we are sick." At least *you* have decided this.

Does the leader think you and the others are sick? His questions and comments may sound like a psychotherapist. What is he trying to do? The leader probably uses techniques and theories of group interaction that have grown out of psychotherapy. But a clear distinction must be made between group psychotherapy and sharing groups of normal people. The former group is composed of persons who must ask the question: "Why do I hurt so much?" The purpose of meetings is to probe deeply into the twisted problems of previous experience, the distortions of present relationships, the inhibition of hope for the future. People who enter such groups are carefully screened by experienced therapists and are often seen individually in addition to weekly group meetings over a long period.

If you are sick, or think that you are, talk to a group leader before you start any sessions. You will find it more comfortable to know *now* if you're starting into a group that is asking your kind of questions.

What Will They Think?

If you and your companions seem to be healthy, why should you talk about yourself? Won't it be better to sit quietly and listen to people who have real problems?

You'll soon find that most of your associates are asking the same questions. So let's reverse the questions. What would *you* think about a person who could share something of himself in a meeting like this? You would probably admire him for his openness and reach out to help him during a hard part of the conversation. He would probably say something with which you could identify. You might even speak up then and say that his sharing was a gift with your name on it.

Gordon was drawn into his group discussion when each person was asked to explain a picture from childhood. Gordon had sketched out four people standing by a duck pond. He said that this was one of the happiest memories from childhood. It was the time that his father took the family to the city park on July fourth.

The group leader asked: "Were there other times when your father took you on outings?"

Gordon: "Well (pause) I guess once or twice more. We never went anywhere as a family. We never went anywhere. I had to find things to do on my own. I never did mix very well."

Allen, another group member, frowned as he listened to this discussion. Then he looked up at Gordon and said: "Say, this helps me understand my nervousness about holidays—or even having fun when I'm at home. My father never did anything but work. I never have done anything but work. My kids ask me why we never go anywhere. How would I know where to take them? I never went anywhere—just like you."

Gordon has made a contribution to Allen's understanding about himself. Allen's analysis of his own experience has helped Gordon to understand his own loneliness and confusion when it is time to have fun. How is it with you? If a group member can make a contribution to your life, could you make a contribution to his? The question about talking or not talking is pointed at personal worth. Don't ask if other people think you have something to say. Ask yourself: "Am I so empty and worthless that I have nothing to contribute to this fellowship?"

A skillful leader will know how to move you through hesitation about self-worth into some significant statement about yourself. He or she may begin a session with an elementary request: "Take the paper and colors before you and draw your childhood home." When each person describes his home, we have begun to know him. It's a socially acceptable way of acquaintance. You won't lose face in the first meeting. Later when you know each other better the request may be more intimate: "Today I would like for you to draw the happiest scene of the past few years" or "Draw something disagreeable."

Sometimes a meeting begins with this question: "Just what do each of you expect to get out of these sessions together?" Now we will begin to know the group goals. Are most people asking a question about sickness, about life, about God, about some task to which they have been assigned? The questions that appear in the first few meetings will define our task together.

Why Are We Here?

Each group will have some unique goals, but generally we can expect some variation on three main purposes. The first of these is support. Healthy people gain confirmation from the comments of others about their attitudes and behavior. You can measure your ideas and feelings against persons who are trying to listen with understanding. They may tell of similar experiences, or interpret your thinking in a better way than you have seen it. That is, they may talk about the strength or weakness of your viewpoint rather than labeling you as good or bad. A group leader is especially important when we start to judge one another. He can suggest terms that are more supportive and less condemning.

Jeannie was very tense in the third meeting. When someone asked if she were hurting, she replied: "I guess so. I mean, all this talk about being honest is getting to me. You see, when I was in undergraduate school, I wasn't really honest. I cheated in some courses. I never could understand math! I hate being a cheat."

"You think you are a cheat?" asked the discussion leader. "Was this a weakness under pressure or do you think this is the way you are all the time?"

"Oh no," replied Jeannie. "In fact, I withdrew from the course while I was still passing and took some biology courses in place of the math courses. We could substitute one for the other. No, I wouldn't say that I am a cheat all the time. But I was bothered about what I did then."

"So you were bothered at the time, and you took appropriate action," he replied. "You did not deserve to pass that course, as you saw it, so you withdrew and got no credit for it. It sounds to me as though you solved your problem at that time." After the leader said this, he hoped that Jeannie might want to go into a discussion of why she was under such pressure in college to pass that particular course. But she seemed so relieved by his interpretation, that he and others just enjoyed her spirit of relaxation. Several people said: "Your face is not so tense now," or "You look around at us as though you belonged."

A normal group of people will realize that they are together for a short period of time to understand themselves better. You will not spend the rest of your life in intimate sharing with people from all walks of life. You are gaining specific support at this time for a common purpose. It may be to do a job better, to confirm or change some ideas about yourself, to be trained for service to others who have problems. Whatever the purpose, this is a short-term gathering that is not basic to your existence. You will probably live a freer and more creative life because of this experience, but you could have existed without it.

On the other hand, a psychotherapy group is essential to the functioning of disturbed, isolated, and lonely people. They may feel that their only comfort is in a weekly session with a doctor and people who understand. Their main support comes from the warmth and guidance of this companionship. Usually the terms of treatment are three months, six months, or a year. Some groups may continue from three to five years, and very inadequate people may meet weekly or monthly for fifteen years.

If you are a normal person who is getting what he needs

from a sharing group, you won't need this particular kind of support forever. But you will learn something about your needs to depend on others and your opportunities to lift the emotional burden of your fellowman. These are valuable lessons for a lifetime.

A second goal of group discussion is insight. As we tell other people what we see in ourselves, they confirm or deny our opinions. Perhaps we have judged ourselves too harshly. Or we may have missed a significant fault that is apparent to others.

A look into ourselves will usually sharpen our identity. We become more aware of ways in which we are like other people and ways in which we are dissimilar. When the sessions are over we can probably measure ourselves and others more accurately.

This contemporary measurement may challenge some opinions that came to us in the past. The hidden assumptions of our family may be revealed in a group that does not share their opinions. We then have a choice of believing what we have been told all our lives or modifying self-perception in the light of adult judgments. Maybe our parents misjudged us because of some of their own problems or perhaps we did not understand what they were trying to tell us. A review of some previous conceptions should be refreshing, whether we become more like those who have molded us. If we continue in one way, it will now be because of an adult affirmation. We will not continue to walk blindly in a childhood past. If on the other hand we make some changes in our attitudes, we will know that it is a responsible decision that is based on consensus rather than our isolated opinion. When we know what people really think of us today, we can realistically review the picture of ourselves and others that was molded in the past.

In this progress of self-understanding, you may or may not talk much about the past. The usual emphasis of a group is upon the here and now. "How are you feeling at *this* moment of time?" is the leader's challenge. Sometimes we need to review the reasons for our present attitudes. This can be done by occasional questions: "When did you first remember hearing that? Who were the important people who talked about that idea?"

Healthy people do not have to tell everything about their past to make some reasonable conclusions about the present. This distinguishes a sharing group from group psychotherapy in which people are very uncomfortable with their attitude toward self and others or who cannot verbalize the way that they feel right now. With very inhibited or double-minded people it is often necessary to dramatize the past so that the painful feelings from yesterday can be connected with present awareness. So, instead of asking for general opinions about our life in the family, the group leader might ask one member to be the child and other members to be brother, sister, mother, and father. The "child" then instructs other members of the family in the way they are to behave and talk as he remembers his own childhood. A specific instance is dramatized, such as father at the dinner table or sister coming home from a dance. As a person recreates the past, his emotional contact with those scenes is renewed. He and others can begin to understand the influence of the past upon the present.

A normal sharing group would not probe so deeply into the roots of sickness. Instead, your group would probably concentrate on the role playing of situations that emphasize personal growth or prepare you for professional service.

In a confrontation group, a ghetto dweller might be asked to play the part of a white policeman, while white members of the session would act as blacks who were being questioned. That is a here and now situation that is aimed at attitude change through personal understanding.

The dramatic presentation of a social or professional problem will usually lead toward another goal of a group. This is some change in attitude and behavior. The sharing of various points of view will improve social skills. We may become more warm, honest, and understanding during typical conflict situations in a family, work, or social life. It may come through the realization by a young man that women are human beings with feelings and rights like his own. They are not trophies for conquest or playmates for the evening. A woman may realize that she is excessively competitive with men in her work. She ascribes to all men the arrogance and prerogatives that she resented in her father, brothers, or other important people in the past. She will certainly be easier to work with, or to live with, when she learns to listen and respond to men without trying to put them down. This will happen when she learns that all men are not trying to lord it over her. They may have as much respect for her as a person as they hope she has for them.

Among young adults, many of the changes in behavior are not dictated by a need to remedy some deficiency in personality. The usual demand is for a more abundant life or skill in some specific task to which you feel called. The "problems" are issues in growth and development. We see this in religiously oriented groups where people want to first experience the meaning of faith, hope, and love. Individuals will also be looking for appropriate expressions of those virtues. How do the members of the group see humility, trust, courage in your life?

A task-oriented group may be seeking definite behavorial change. Sensitivity sessions for the supervisors of migrant workers were necessary in order to dissipate patronizing attitudes. The boss had to confront his own need to dominate the workers and also understand the workers' reluctance to step out and make decisions for themselves. It was only after a series of meetings between supervisors and workers that both groups could use a new company program for their mutual benefit.

Sharing groups are often a prerequisite in professional training. Graduate students may meet with a supervisor to talk over their gut reactions with clients or staff in a hospital clinic or court room. Volunteers for foreign or domestic social service may go through a laboratory of human situations: the isolation and doubt of service with a different race or nationality, the fixed opinions of supervisors in distant lands who seldom confront their equals who have different ideas, the frustration of a desire to help when people may not share your goals or mistrust your motives. These are unusual challenges which take emotional preparation for professional service.

The higher the challenge, the greater our vulnerability. A routine task may not require much self-examination. The shuffling of papers in an office may be done without much training in sharing. But when we get into service that requires personal commitment, we must know ourselves and others. Without wisdom and understanding, the cause is jeopardized. This was dramatized in the civil rights struggle of the 1960s. The leaders of nonviolence were careful to train their demonstrators. A group member would act as a belligerent segregationist who might spit in the face of a demonstrator, slap him, insult him, provoke him in any possible way. When the demonstrator had learned to control his temper, he was ready for the real thing.

In contrast, a white graduate student in one group exclaimed: "Man, if a policeman did this to me I would murder him!" It took many sessions for that aggressive and brave young man to bear frustration. Finally he learned self-control through the blacks and poor whites who shared their own sufferings and hostilities with him. They taught him how to bear his own burden of rage and hurt while he attempted to carry the burdens of others.

Are All the Cards on the Table?

If people discover a good deal about themselves through these sharing sessions, how can they know what to expect beforehand? So far we have dealt with the general expectations of a beginning group. As the group forms, we may be in for some surprises as a specific issue emerges. You may not have thought that *this* was in your mind or was the intention of anyone else. But here is a hidden agenda that may be almost accidentally discovered. Sometimes you see it in yourself, sometimes in members of the group, and sometimes in the leader. If that which has been hidden can be acknowledged, the group can be stronger. You may have learned something about yourself that is like a revelation. Certainly you would not have admitted this if the persons whom you now trust had not been a mirror of yourself.

If a man cannot stand to look into the mirror, he will

withdraw. That's a safe and sane procedure. Come back again when you are ready for this kind of experience, or find the group that is asking your kind of questions. All the cards are going to come out on the table somewhere, and it should be by the rules of a game to which you agree.

As we get close to self-disclosure, a decision has to be made. Am I going to talk with these people, with someone in private, or not at all?

Behind this is the question: "What's special about this kind of experience?" Why should a person find value in this sensitive session that is not available in many other relationships of life?

We seek an answer to these questions as we decide for or against sharing, and we also ask the same questions as our feelings for the group increases. As we get into the process of experiencing with others, we want to know what is happening to us. Why does this context produce particular kinds of self-understanding or awareness of others? This is the first series of questions that come up in the mid-part of group involvement, "What is a group experience?"

chapter 3
what is a group experience?

Whatever the purposes of a particular group meeting, some basic bonding of people with one another is desired. This thinking together, mutual awareness, common understanding is all caught up in a general phrase, "group experience." Somehow, the objectives of the sessions together are not achieved until people are convinced that they are a "group." But just what does that word mean?

"Group" has a very special meaning when we place it with an adjective like "encounter" or "sharing." Then it must meet the qualifications that Paul Hare has presented in his *Handbook of Small Group Research*. Out of years of experience in working with people who banded together for common purposes, Dr. Hare and others found the following ingredients in a dynamic group experience.

(1) A "group" begins with interaction. There is a deliberate concentration upon the way we talk, the person or persons to whom we address ourselves, the way in which we sit, the place that we sit, the movements that we make, the expressions on our face.

For the time that we are together, observations about interaction will be crucial. We deliberately heighten our awareness of gestures, tone of voice, speech implications to learn how we relate with different kinds of people.

This will be a new way of relating for some of us. It

will be especially significant for the person who is not accustomed to listening while others are speaking. Instead, he is thinking of what to say next. He only follows his own train of thought. One of the first books on group process in business was concerned with this problem. In *Human Relations,* Hugh Kabot and Joseph Kahl introduce the cartoon of two persons in conversation. The first was gaily chattering to his companion. The companion sat contently in his chair, headless. His head was behind the chair, wrapped in thought. What was he going to say when the first speaker had stopped?

"Pay attention!" is the first sign that a group is forming. We emerge from self-preoccupation to take note of the way that people hear us and we hear them.

(2) A group has direction. This is the purpose of asking: "What are we here for?" The major purpose is a process rather than a product. You are learning ways by which you can relate with more accuracy and sympathy. You are hoping that others will help you to see how you make decisions, why you think of others and yourself as you do. These are steps to self-understanding. We go through this experience to understand the way that we structure our own thinking. We also pick up clues that will help us identify the ways by which people move closer together or defend themselves against intimacy.

The emphasis upon process will define a sensitivity group or theme-centered interaction. On the other hand, a group in industry or professional life might be called together to produce something. There may be a special problem to be solved, an organization to be formed, a social crisis to be met. In such a group, some emphasis upon process will be necessary to increase understanding and the awareness of other points of view, but the success of meeting will be determined by the production of a plan of organization, a design for a building, a recommendation for city planning.

You may be so accustomed to a product oriented group that you are restless with an interpersonal orientation. A "groupy" group seems a waste of time. What is being produced except talk? The question will help us to clarify goals and also determine the health of the people in this meeting.

The goal of a productive group is not talk for its own sake. Only in psychotherapy groups is it essential that each person say what he is feeling. Sick people have been so repressed that they cannot express themselves without pain and uncertainty. Much time and attention is necessary for them to state what is going on inside. When they have begun to say it like it is, healing has occurred.

In a group full of neurotics, there may be many words without meaning. The person who seeks self-glory is fascinated with his own voice. The leader must help each person to think through what he is saying. What is his purpose in talking this way? What signs of authenticity are there in his voice, his movements, his style of life? Is his verbalization consistent with what we know of his motivation and manner? Through continual challenges, the leader and group participants move each member toward a closer identification of word with deed, head with heart.

In a more normal group, we can concentrate more upon the results of telling. We do not need to spend much time in the probing of reasons for a person's declaration of intent. If he says that he will do thus and so when he gets back home, we can share our experiences of a similar nature instead of asking in detail about the reasons for this particular plan of action. We are more interested in the *fruits* of words rather than their *roots*.

Talking is only a means to an end. The same is true of closeness and cohesiveness. These are elements of understanding, but not the goals of a short term group. We meet under stated conditions for a brief period of time in order that our effectiveness in the larger world may be increased. We want to learn how to be more warm in our family, more understanding in our business, more friendly in our society. A group cohesiveness is a temporary means of experiencing that which should be stronger in our regular life among people with whom we have an enduring association.

If a person gets "hooked" on "sharing," he will hang on to the temporary group as though it were his permanent family. Dr. Carl Rogers has noted the frequency with which some persons move up and down the coast of California from one sharing workshop to another. Dr. Irvin Yalom found that three of the members in one of his marathon groups had just completed another marathon group. This has led to a new clinical syndrome, "the group addict."

(3) A group sets up and abides by boundaries and limitations for their interpersonal relationships. Questions of confidentiality must be settled. This is the beginning of trust. Physical boundaries between people are established. The usual rule is that one person may verbally express anger to another person, but is to refrain from pushing, hitting, spitting, or biting.

More subtle norms develop around the amount of sharing that we will do in this particular group. Some persons talk a great deal with an outside group about the behavior of persons in the group. One person criticizes another behind his back. How much of this behavior should be brought out in the group discussion?

Attendance and promptness are norms that measure the commitment of individuals to the group. Infrequent attendance by an individual is a sign of something. We should ask about it. A drop in attendance by a large percentage of the group is another symptom that should be investigated. What has happened?

These norms can serve as calibrations on an emotional thermometer. We "read" the group temperature by the limitations which they observe.

(4) A set of roles are soon established in any collection of individuals that is moving toward a group experience. We soon observe that one person is dominant in discussions with the leader. He tells about himself and makes interpretations of the group. He asks questions of the leader and offers suggestions.

Other persons soon become known for their passivity. Their usual movement is a nodding of the head. They are the audience for the dominant person who either takes over from the leader or is in dialogue with him.

In time, antagonists may appear. Two or more persons may spar with each other or gang up on the leader. Some of the tension generated by their conflict is relieved by the clowns, the humorists on the edge of tragedy.

The leader's helpers usually emerge as the group develops. These persons do not share much about themselves, but are able to summarize what has occurred and to raise provocative questions or offer sympathetic remarks.

The presentation of these roles is important to self-understanding. As a person demonstrates his position in a group, other members can evaluate this to see if it is consistent with the way that an individual views himself.

A member of the Association of Group Psychotherapists, Dr. Jacob Christ, has noted the different behavior of a person in a variety of roles. The same individual may act one way as a student, another has a husband, a third as a participant in group therapy. It is necessary for us to ask if the role assumed at one time in therapy is consistent with the person's behavior in the home or in the office or at the club.

When members ask these questions of each other, a group is moving toward solidarity. Instead of all questions coming from the leader, people are speaking directly to each other. They are expressing specific interest in what this person has to say in the context of the feelings of others in this group.

(5) When people are speaking directly to each other with understanding, we have a network of interpersonal attraction. We know that the group now has real meaning. People are not talking just to talk, nor are they sharing just to share. They are now speaking with understanding of themselves and others. They are being accepted as they are by others.

When this occurs, we have some of the signs of a successful group which have been documented in Dr. Irvin Yalom's *The Theory and Practice of Group Psychotherapy* through his questions to participants in group psychotherapy. People who have been in a successful group say that they feel accepted by the persons who were with them. This leads the participants to be more aware of themselves and of others.

The participants also see many similarities to each other in successful groups. Accurate measurement indicates that people are more like each other than they are different. Isolation is reduced, and empathy is increased.

In successful groups, people are specific and accurate in their references to each other. Their personal assessment skills are enhanced. Because of these accurate comments, a person is willing to be influenced by what others say. They *really* know him as he is.

When a desire to support others is combined with an accurate assessment of others, group communication increases self-esteem and realistic evaluation. This is one of the major benefits of a group discussion. After these discussions, you may realize that your views of self and others have been corrected in a number of ways. If you went into the group with a low evaluation of self, you probably distorted the group's reaction to you, or you decided that the group was of no real value to you. When your interpretations were challenged, you had to be stubborn and reject the group or look seriously at the possibility of distortion. If you found that the group was accurate, there probably would be some shift in your self-image.

The people who shift the most in a group are those who attain popularity. You will notice that a person who can express his emotions freely will soon receive many comments. People are eager to help those who want to help themselves. The subject under discussion may be very unattractive or morally reprehensible. But the person is willing to tell about himself, and you feel that this is enough to call out your concern.

In contrast, the person who hides his talent in the ground

will have little to show when the program is completed. He has not revealed himself and has therefore been neglected. On some occasions the group might center attention upon him briefly, but they were soon discouraged and moved to those who would offer more. It is soon apparent that we do not get much more out of a group than we are willing to place in it.

What do we usually receive from a cohesive banding of people? Three rewards are support, suppression, and the understanding of problems. We are offered acceptance and approval for our moves toward stronger affirmation of healthy tendencies in ourselves. Because of the values we find in ourselves, we can suppress some of the undesirable qualities of personality that have hampered us in the past. The rewards of openness, trust, and warmth are greater than the lures of secrecy, distrust, and manipulation. We also receive specific understanding of our ways of thinking and the steps by which people go through the solution of problems. With this understanding we can approach our difficulties with new confidence and provide wise counsel to those who lean upon us.

Groping for a Group

The group that supplies support and understanding will be promoted by those who are "in" and sought by those who are "out." In a college or hospital which emphasizes group work, the word will soon spread for or against a particular group. One is sought after. The members tell their friends of the great experiences in sharing and understanding. Other people wonder why their collection of individuals in one room has never coalesced. They are still groping toward something that is called a "group."

Much of the groping could become grouping if the five characteristics of cohesion were developed. The beginning point would be concentration upon each other and a leader who can help us interpret what we see in each other. Second, some understanding of purpose would emerge out of the first few meetings. If the question, "What are we here for?" is repeated for a dozen sessions, then there is merely groping. Sometimes people leave one group and join another before the first one can achieve a clear sense of purpose and direction. For example, a group of writers met weekly during a summer to discuss their material. It was soon apparent that a lack of self-understanding and inhibitions were cramping the style of most of the writers. As the people began to understand this, several pushed for full confessions of moral failures, deep analysis of parental relationships, open discussions of marriage difficulties. Most of the members objected to this and said that they wanted to discuss only the parts of their lives that were related to their writing assignment at the present time. After four sessions, three members left in disgust. They felt that the other members were inhibited persons who did not want to "really share." These three joined with some others in a local university to undertake therapy under the direction of a clinical psychologist. The writers continued their meetings with a growing sense of satisfaction. Each man learned something about his profession from the material brought in by others, and also was encouraged to talk about himself when there was a "hang-up" in the way that he wrote. The task of the group, to improve writing through self-understanding, was clarified and accepted.

This example demonstrates the third characteristic of

successful groups, which is the development and adherence to limitations in interpersonal relationships. There is a sense of discipline in an active, growing group.

In time, people are free enough to show some major characteristics of their relationships in the group experience. This is when we know the role that a person plays with others. His aggression or his passivity become evident. This is often the major contribution of a group to an individual. He goes away with a clearer understanding of how he relates to other people. He identifies the "come on" that will set him up for an aggressive or passive relationship. He also begins to sense his own movement toward one type of relationship. As one member said: "I can now see myself while I am in action."

When we reach this awareness of ourselves and others, we incorporate the fifth characteristic of a group. This is the ability to see ourselves in a relationship without the usual alarms of blame or striving for praise. We accurately see the characteristic motion of this or that person. We are satisfied to know how things are. We may be concerned about the way that things should be, but now we can begin with a realistic assessment of where we stand with each other.

These are the characteristics of a group. But what is the process by which we become cohesive? This is the question of technique, to which we turn in the next chapter.

chapter 4
how do we begin?

First sessions can be fun, if you don't take yourself too seriously. You will probably begin with some psychological warm-up exercises. People are as stiff in the early stages of conversation as they are physically tight in the early morning. It takes a little while for the warmth of human relations to warm up the meeting.

An imaginative leader will get things going in a socially acceptable way. He may ask where you are from and why you are here. This will bring out some of the questions that set the direction, limits, and goals for the group. When each person has spoken, the leader may ask if there is any consensus on the purpose of this gathering: "Who can say why most of us are here?"

There may be a more active beginning through the drawing of pictures, the molding of clay, the leading of people in physical exercises. We can dramatize the psychological term "trust" by dividing the group into pairs and asking one person in each pair to close his or her eyes. The partner then leads the "blind" person for five minutes. This may sound like a very elementary parlor game, but you will be surprised by the statements that people make after everyone has done this. You will sit back down in a circle, and each person will be asked what he experienced as he was being led.

There are many interesting ways to get going toward a group. You may not need these exercises if the people have come together for a common purpose and have some previous mandate for their discussion. If you are in that kind of group, everybody will "get down to business" in a hurry. The "business" will be defined by the reasons given you for attending these sessions.

If the instructions for your coming were not specific, you won't start very fast without some warm-up exercises. In fact, the group might be frustrated by a leader who thinks that he is acting as the therapist for a bunch of sick people. He may have been influenced by the psychiatric practice of group therapy, in which a leader takes little action in any group discussion. Or he may have read the early works of Carl Rogers, which emphasize individual initiative. Some leaders interpret "nondirective" as non-productive and respond only on rare occasions to some general feeling they have about the group.

It's quite frustrating for people to sit and stare at the leader or at each other for an hour. You have probably heard of groups that began that way. The result is usually some expression of irritation or frustration from persons in the circle. The leader then nods and asks: "I wonder why you are feeling so hostile." You might answer: "Because we have no leadership and are wasting our time!" An extractive leader will be pleased by your anger. He assumes that anger is valuable for its own sake and that this is the major content of any group experience. If you are enraged, he will consider you "authentic." With this encouragement, other people will have begun to express their hostilities toward you, the leader, other members in the group, family, the boss, and associates.

The extractive leader will then believe that his job is well done. He has frustrated people to the point that they begin to be aggressive with each other. He keeps pushing people toward each other in a way that arouses anger. This psychological crowding has a predictable result, fighting. It has been demonstrated repeatedly in colonies of rats who are crowded together in too small a space for comfortable living. Rats who would ordinarily give each other living room must now fight for a little piece of freedom. In the same way, a leader may exploit our natural defense of life space by creating artificial conditions of psychological crowding.

This method is considered valuable by some experts in the group psychotherapy of psychotic and chronically neurotic individuals. Such people are so emotionally inhibited that they need some artificial means of expression. They are not self-starters.

On the other hand, a group of normal people will be irritated by the frustrating silence of a leader or his loaded comments that goad people against each other. We realize that this kind of interaction is inappropriate in society and unnecessary for self-actualized individuals. We can talk freely and appropriately about ourselves if some acceptable device for sharing is provided in the first few sessions.

What will you do if the leader is elusive and extractive? You might go home after the first session. The "drop-out" problem is chronic among nondirective groups. Or you could assume some leadership in the first or second session by suggesting one or more of the warm-up exercises that help people enjoy each other as they get acquainted. If the paid leader of the group or some member asks why you and others are taking the lead, you can give the psychologically valid answer that natural leadership fills a vacuum in any group. Since the paid leader *seems* to be permissive, how could he object to self-determination of methods by which these people will interact with each other?

Why Work as a Group?

Whether your leader is active or passive, someone will ask, "Why are we here?" or "State the purposes for which you have been assigned to this gathering." As the reasons for participation become clear to you, another question will come up: Do all of these things need to be discussed in a group? We can tell from the words and actions of some people that they surely need a caring fellowship. They tell of their shyness around people, their fears of rejection, their loneliness and despair. But others, perhaps including you, have questions that might be answered alone or with one other person. Why not figure for yourself the usual problems of belief and conduct? In a religiously oriented group, some people may ask why their thoughts of God and fellowmen must be shared. Is it not enough to speak alone with the Lord? Why should we check out our moral dilemmas with anyone else when prayer, Bible study, and confession are available?

One answer to these questions was worked out in the "great awakening" of religion in colonial America. The Reverend Jonathan Edwards found that many of his people could not feel what they believed, or believe what they were feeling. The head and the heart were not together. The result was an unrealistic picture of self and the world. People could not accurately picture what was happening to them. Nor did they know how to make the teachings of their family, society, and religion a part of their own lives.

Pastor Edwards' solution was to invite the townspeople to his home on afternoons and evenings for a discussion of their feelings about his Sunday sermons. If their hearts were strangely warmed, he asked them to speak of this and offered some guidance and interpretations. In addition to these group sessions, he met individually with those who wanted to know if their emotional stirrings were signs of a true awakening of religion. Others came to ask how they might personally experience the teachings they had come to believe.

People began to be in touch with their own feelings as a result of these group and individual meetings. They felt truly alive for the first time, for now they were open to whatever was happening to them and could explain their experiences in words that the minister and church could understand.

We are using the same theory and techniques to solve the same problem today, both in secular or religious circles. Rollo May has written of the struggle of modern man to bring love and will together. In his *Love and Will,* May discusses the dilemma of people who are out of touch with their feelings. His patients read every new book on sexual techniques and hope that "experiencing" will make them alive. But they are psychologically dead because of emotional inhibitions. They need discussions in which the meaning of key words is connected to their personal lives. This is also accomplished in a group where people ask us: "Where did you learn to say things like that?" or "Put into words what you are experiencing." Or we may be challenged: "You don't act like what you say; you say that no one can reach you, but you get stiff when any of us criticize you."

These and other comments are aimed at a basic goal of every group, to bring head and heart together. We need a conscious realization of who we are and how we feel. There must be some testing of our explanations against the impressions of others. It is in the group that we understand the expectations that others have of us, their estimates of our worth, our own ability to know the ways in which we are like others or different from them. This experience with others will sharpen our social skills, increase the realism of our judgments, shape up our identity.

How Far Can We Go?

You may wonder if all of these values can come out of a few group meetings. No, the job is not done in a weekend marathon or in periodic meetings for two or three months. The purpose of short- or long-term therapy is to get us started in the right direction. We may need to unlock some secret doors to ourselves, use some new words in explaining our moods or behavior, see how others respond to feelings that are common to people of our age.

A group helps to bring love and will together, but it cannot meet all the expectations that some people bring to our first meetings. You will notice that one or two persons will try to tell everything immediately. They are much too anxious for growth. Personal insight and development may take surprising leaps during group experience, but solid results take time.

Don't outrun yourself. Say as much as you can assimilate. An alert leader will slow down the discussion if you are moving beyond your own powers of understanding what you are saying, or pouring out more emotion than a group can bear. There are definite limits to the changes that occur in short-term group sessions, so take what you can in each hour and lay something aside for the next.

Mr. Cates was anxious to "get all that he could out of the group." After the leader had said in the first session that people should feel free to express themselves, Mr. Cates began to speak.

MR. CATES: "I am certainly glad to hear this. I understand from what has been said that most of us have entered this group to get to know ourselves better. Of course, we already know each other superficially by being in graduate school. But I don't think that we really get to know the problems of other people in the courses that we take. Take me for example. Everybody thinks that we are a loving couple. Well, we do look good when we are out with some of you at a party, but my wife is very inhibited; I mean she doesn't really enjoy sex in marriage. Huh, I don't mean that she is enjoying it anywhere else—I, huh, mean—"

LEADER: "You are saying that freedom of expression between husband and wife is one of the areas that you would like for us to explore during the twelve sessions that we are together. Is that right?"

MR. CATES: "Yes. Now me, I have no trouble talking about myself. I believe that I can express myself anytime, anywhere. But now with my wife it is different. Like I was saying she—"

LEADER: "You say that you are able to express yourself very freely in all sorts of circumstances. This is something that is more possible for some of us than others. How is it with some of the rest of you? Do you find it easy to talk about yourself in many different situations?" (look around the group)

Several members began to say that they were not so free in expressing themselves. The leader asked the circumstances under which they were not free and the circumstances under which they were free. The rest of the session was spent in a discussion of times when we can or cannot tell exactly what we are thinking.

Why did the leader interrupt Mr. Cates's attempt to speak more about the sexual inhibitions of his wife? The group was just forming and there was no common bond of understanding which would bear that deep a revelation. An intimate disclosure would have to wait for another meeting.

These limitations may seem strange when leaders are usually saying "feel free to express anything." But in a group that emphasizes understanding, the freedom is related to responsibility. How much can a person say now that he and the groups members will be able to assimilate?

Most leaders are really trying to tell us: "Be exact and honest." They do not expect you to say everything that comes into your mind. They do expect you to tell one thing "straight" at a time. That is, lay aside some of the superficial padding in talking about yourself. Say what you are thinking without distortion.

Mr. Cates learned this lesson in a later meeting. He was always making up excuses for his actions, including the things that he did in the group. In one meeting, someone noticed that he had changed the place where he usually was seated. He formerly sat between two men. Today he was seated between two attractive young ladies.

Mr. Cates: "Well, I just thought that they should have some company [laugh], then there wasn't any other place for me to sit down. I thought that it would be a gracious thing for me to sit by them because they had that seat vacant between them—"

Mr. Merton: "Did you really? I saw you get up from your customary seat and go over to sit by Jane when she first came in. When Audrey came in, you asked her to sit down by you. I don't care where you sit, but I do think that excuses are unnecessary. Why don't you just say that you wanted to talk with these attractive people?"

Mr. Cates: "Oh, I am sure that they are very attractive. Of course I enjoy sitting by them. I did not mean to say that it was not a pleasure."

Mr. Merton: "But you tried to make us think that circumstances forced you to sit by them. Actually, it was your choice. Is there anything wrong with sitting with them? You just said that it was a pleasure. Why can't you affirm what you want to do without having to make excuses and blaming it on circumstances?"

The deepest lesson for Mr. Cates to learn is that he can speak directly about his needs without having to protect himself on all occasions. This is different from his mistaken belief that a person is really free if he can talk about a wide range of intimate subjects. The revelation of family or business or community secrets does not necessarily indicate personal growth in a group. They would really be acceptable only under the strict rules of confidentiality that operate among sick people in group psychotherapy. They are to discuss *nothing* that occurs in a group session with anyone else, nor are they to discuss the group experience with anyone else in the group after the session is completed for that day. They say much more about themselves and others because they are in great need of help. At the same time, the rules are more strict because of the damage that might result from the exposure of socially unacceptable information.

In a healthier group, you will have to decide something about confidentiality. If you never plan to see these people again, and know them only by their first names, you can probably say a good deal without risk of exposure back home. But what if you have to work with some of these folks for the next few years? How much will you say of your previous opinions about them and the present evaluation that some associates have about them? You may be too close for comfortable disclosure of private opinions.

The composition and purpose of the group will determine the rules that you make. If you are together for self-knowledge, then a rule of confidentiality will be necessary for any deep discussion of personal issues. If the group is more "task oriented," you can agree that each session will begin with a theme, a problem situation, a case for discussion. You will be telling how a problem impresses you and others may comment on the way you come across to them. But the discussion will be centered on mutual solution of a common professional problem. Confidentiality will not be a big issue.

Why make rules? If people learn to trust each other, won't they be confidential without anyone telling them that this is necessary? Yes, but we need time to learn how to trust one another. Adults should not be naive. Some people can keep a confidence, and others will gossip. There will have to be some testing of each other.

The rules are necessary in the beginning to shape our goals and control our anxiety. They are like a contract. We will work for these purposes, put in this much of ourselves, expect this much of others. If we enter voluntarily, we have a right to know how and where we are going. Without some mutual commitment in the beginning, there will be little sharing that will be realistic. Commitment comes before confidence.

The Ins and Outs

Verbal contracts sign us into a group. A person who is unwilling to share the contract signs out. We start with definite terms for those who are going to stay in.

Once the covenant is made, you will notice that some people move themselves into the circle more readily than others. It appears that some people are going to get all that they can out of these sessions, so they are putting in as much of themselves as possible.

Others are more reticent. They sit in the circle each day, but no one is sure of their thoughts. You might be one of them on some occasion. You may be bored by the interchanges or convinced that you will not go out on a limb like somebody else has done. Or you may lack commitment to the whole process of open self-inquiry. You are not moved by what is said to speak for yourself.

In the beginning hours or days of a group, the in-out question is prominent. We observe the movement of others and we debate in ourselves, shall I keep my thoughts to myself or tell these people what I am feeling?

An early solution to the problem might be a warm relationship with someone outside of the sharing hour. You might talk freely to your roommate, spouse, or companion. You try out self-disclosure under conditions that you can control. If the results are beneficial, you may be encouraged to risk more in a larger group setting.

You may decide that self-disclosure is not worth it with these people. You're satisfied with what you know about yourself from conversations back home or with husband or wife.

Of course you may be satisfied with what you know about yourself, but how much of you must be known by the people with whom you are going to work in the future? Is there something about yourself that would be of benefit to others? Is your stand on some personal question necessary for the success of some enterprise? Have people seen how you react in an intimate experience? How can they have confidence in you or know how to relate without your self-disclosure?

The Top and the Bottom

While you and others are thinking about the ins and outs, another part of the group interaction will emerge. This is the process of competition. Who is going to be heard? How will you get others to understand what you are saying? What will you do about interruptions?

One or more persons will soon appear as dominant. He or she will take the lead in discussions, talk about himself or offer interpretations of the remarks of others. In time, you will notice that you or others can maintain a position with strength for five or ten minutes. You adequately answer the questions that are put to you and face various interpretations with realistic rejoinders. It is plain that for that period of time you, or the person that talks this way, is getting attention and admiration.

At the other extreme, you or others may be on the bottom. You say very little, and what you said yesterday is not remembered today by anyone. What you or some other person says "on the bottom" will sound dismal, distressing, despairing. There just doesn't seem to be much hope. It's not just a feeling of inadequacy, it's *real* inadequacy, you think.

Self-doubt is made worse by superior interpretations from a strong group member. This person says things that you should have seen. He is sensitive to feelings that you didn't catch. In fact, you may not think that you are catching on at all. The group is passing you by. You would like to stay with them, but nothing fits together right now.

If you are on the bottom, rise up and say so. A sharing group is to weep with those who weep and rejoice with those that rejoice. There is a place for both extremes. You may be surprised and somewhat comforted to learn that others share your discomfort. Several people may say: "Well, I'm not sure of where we are going," "This has not done me any good so far," "It seems like two or three do all the talking and the rest of us are not sure of what is going on." Then you will not feel so bad on the bottom. You may find that you are in on the ground floor with some other puzzled people. Out of this discussion may come some clear awareness of who is dominant and when, who is submissive and under what circumstances. This will be a useful discussion for young adults, who are in the midst of competition in life. You're mobilizing energy to get ahead and this is sometimes at the expense of others. Or you may have found that it's too expensive to you. Now is a good time to discuss that problem.

The Near and the Far

After some awareness of competition the group may move ahead toward compassion. You will then be more aware of those who are more near to you and those that are more distant from you in any group discussion. Each of you will also be concerned about anyone who is missing for a particular session. What has happened? Concern has moved beyond self-disclosure to mutual support and understanding.

Mutual understanding does not mean continued closeness. You may feel warmer toward a person during today's discussion than you were yesterday or will be tomorrow. Feelings for members of the circle will vary with the subject under discussion or the way their personalities strike you. At times you may say: "I have not been very interested in what you have had to say until now, but I really get with you on this subject."

Continued closeness is only required in mutual friendship or family relations. The people who have come together for these sessions may or may not be on intimate terms in the future. Your investment among these people is for a specified period of time under controlled conditions.

During this time, you will learn much about yourself as you observe the distance between you and others on certain occasions. Some of your remarks do not turn on anyone, whereas others are sure to get immediate attention.

You will have a more accurate picture of what annoys you in some people and attracts you to others, for you will be measuring attention and interest during the group discussion.

When you and others begin to think this way, you are really in a group. You are ready to define what it means for you to be together.

chapter 5
what happens when i fail?

Healthy people are looking more for competence than for cure in a group discussion. You probably have most of what it takes to do a good job. What you need is some confirmation of your strengths and weaknesses for loving and working. You want to know more about yourself so that service to others will be more effective.

This is different from a psychotic or neurotic person's search for cure through group psychotherapy. He is very aware that something is wrong. Blame may have been projected on others or distorted in the self. There have been many failures in life, and the person is uncertain of his ability to love and be loved. Group discussions must be handled delicately. These people have been hurt so often that they generalize one mistake into a conviction of total failure. When they do one good thing, the entire group must support them, and the leader offers congratulations. This is why therapy groups for narcotic addicts will literally applaud when one member tells a good thing about himself.

You might like to hear some applause in your group, but it's not necessary. You already have enough acceptance in life to talk of intimate matters without continual demonstrations of group support. You can make some distinctions between a failure in one area of life and total failure as a person. For example, one unsuccessful love affair does not cancel your desirability as a love object.

But there may be times that you *feel* totally unworthy. There are moments of bitter reproach and days of doubt.

Should you feel this way about yourself? This is a question for group discussion. This usually starts with some confessions of a feeling of failure. With a little help you can usually define the time and place that were associated with guilt or depression. Just what was it that made you feel so bad?

Bob was accused by a fellow member of "sailing through everything." The group thought that he was able to study every subject in graduate school with no thoughts of academic or emotional difficulties of his fellows.

"Not so," said the bright young fellow. "I have a devil of a time with statistics." When people asked about his ability and grades in math, he replied that in his first years of college there had been no problems. Other students rebuked him for taking class time. They had not solved the elementary problems and were desperately in need of help.

"I felt like a jerk," Bob continued, "so I guess that I have always stumbled over my guilt whenever I came up against math after that."

This strong student did not feel that he was *worthless* because of his inability to sense the needs of fellow students or his present difficulties with a guilt-related subject. But how would he feel if his father continually told him: "Every man in our family has been good in math. What kind of a man are you? I had always thought that you would become an engineer. Why can't you apply yourself?"

Derogatory speeches build up strong feelings around isolated failures in performance. You or someone in the group may have those feelings. Large conclusions are drawn from small incidents. You may have been rebuked so often for little things that you have now decided that you are a little person. In the back of your mind are childhood warnings: "You are the worst person I have ever known," "Why can't you ever do anything right?" "What is wrong with you?" "Why can't you have ambitions like your brother?"

The value of a group discussion is to show the difference between the voices from the past and the reaction of your comrades in the present. The incidents will be the same, but the interpretations may show vivid contrasts. That which seemed so self-defeating in the eyes of a parent, aunt, or brother may be of little consequence to the people who sit around you now.

When you begin to talk about event and interpretation you are getting into the ABCs of personal understanding. A is the action, great or small. B is your belief about the action. That belief is strongly influenced by what you have been told when you were younger. Now you can test your assumption against people of your own age who may or may not agree with your conclusions. That which may have seemed to be a failure in the past is little more than a normal occurrence to people who share with you. You may have a thought that your failures in the past were a sign of total failure as a person. You think that talk about this in the group will add to your condemnation. So you assume that it is best to be quiet and hide your past. C is the consequence of a change in belief and will be evidenced in a new pattern of behavior or thinking.

You may be surprised to find that all of your past mistakes do not add up to complete failure in the eyes of your contemporaries. A thirty-five-year-old lawyer told of self-accusations when he defended some clients who were accused of cheating or stealing. "I can't get rid of the thought that I was once the same way. I cheated on some tests in the school of business. I just couldn't understand the work. Of course, I didn't want to go into business anyway, but that was my mother's wish ever since my father had died and left the business to me. I guess that I have failed her in more than one way."

"How have you failed?" asked a businessman in the group. "Oh" replied the lawyer, "I wouldn't take over the business. It just wasn't the thing that I was interested in. I left the school of business and transferred to the school of law. I guess my mother has gotten over that, but I still feel bad sometimes—like when I remember what I did on some of those courses."

Several members of the group then commented that the lawyer had solved several problems at one time. He had dropped a course of study in which he had no interest and in which he had done some cheating. It was a sensible decision. At the same time, he felt guilty about a different course of action from that required by mother. He had not really lived up to her expectations. "Should you have taken over the business?" said one member.

"No," said the lawyer. "I made the best decision, but I was taught family loyalty and all that sort of thing. I care about my mother and uncles, of course, and I think that they respect my work. But that was a hard time in my life

—back when I left business school—and I guess there is a general sense of guilt associated with a decision against my family. I really did feel like a worm then."

If you feel like a worm, you will burrow deeper into the darkness so that no one will step on you. But if you come up to the surface, you may find that you are suffering as much from isolation as you are from the act that made you feel so small.

Sometimes a devastating act in the past may be too much for group discussion. You may want some private time with the leader to say what you are thinking while the group is talking. One young lady lingered after a group session to tell the counselor: "I was really thinking while Jane was talking about the break-up of her engagement. I think I am very much like her. I am really afraid to commit myself to one man. I know what it comes from and would like to talk privately about it.

"When I was fourteen, my girl friend and I were walking home when a man stopped his car and made some obscene remarks to us. We both ran, but the man got between me and my girl friend. He tried to molest me. When another car came by, he was frightened and drove away.

"I never told a soul except my girl friend. My mother and father would have died if they had known it happened to me." The counselor interrupted: "Why would they have died?" "Well, because they are so anxious that I should be pure. If they knew about that ugly thing, they would think that I was ruined for life."

"Are you?" asked the counselor.

"Oh no," said the young lady. "Nothing really happened. But then I felt so ashamed. Shouldn't I?"

The counselor replied: "What I am feeling is isolation

from your family. An understanding mother and father would have wanted to protect you and comfort you after such an experience. Am I to understand that your parents were not that way?"

"Well, now that I think about it, I guess that they might have taken my side. But I'm not sure. They were very strict and often blamed me for things that I did not do. But I guess that I would forgive—that is, I would understand—if this happened to one of my friends."

"Well," replied the counselor, "I would think that a good father could help by explaining that not all men are like the one man that you met at that early age. Have you talked with any mature man about this before?"

"No," she answered, "I guess that I always thought a father would condemn me. Maybe my father would, but I see that you don't, and I think that I get your point about generalizing. That is, uh, don't be afraid of all men because of that one."

The ease with which this young lady came to a sensible conclusion may sound extraordinary. But we should remember that she has spent an hour in thinking through her past and is a healthy person. In contrast, we should look for slower insight from persons who are deeply disturbed and have many blocks in the way of realistic conclusions. In those cases, secrets come out slowly, and there are many bypasses and distortions.

In a therapy group for troubled people, failures are admitted with more hesitation and anguish. But you would be surprised at the depth of revelations that can be accepted by a group. As a group grows, people can tell some horrifying stories about themselves without experiencing isolation from others in the room. In time we really learn to care enough for each other to bear these burdens of self-contempt and shame.

Whether our sense of failure is gross or microscopic, we can test our self-assumptions in a group setting. This does not mean that we tell everything about ourselves, but it does mean that we follow up a new thought with some change of attitude. The young lady in the previous illustration was unwilling to share specifics with the group, but she could use the meeting to develop more warmth and trust with young men. If she can begin to relate to them as human beings rather than as a menace from the past, she will have taken action that is consistent with a new interpretation of herself.

The consequences of a change of belief is the final process in ABC thinking. We have examined our assumptions about a specific action and now we are ready to try a different attitude or redirect an activity. Now the girl who had been so frightened of men in the past may look at them more directly, talk more openly about herself, respond with warmth to their approval and affection.

The Fading of Fulfillment

Failure seems to be a fear in every group. But we would make a mistake to look only to inadequate people for this sense of dread. Actually, the first talk about inadequacies may come from the most outwardly adequate persons. These are individuals with an insatiable desire to be recognized. In many instances their talents are impressive and their work with others is appreciated. But they ceaselessly strive for approval. Others are put down in their search for recognition. The only satisfaction in life seems to be reward from those in authority.

These people with high achievement motivation are the first to complain of isolation from others. As you listen to them, you will wonder why they are unhappy. Life has been so good to them. They have enjoyed recognition and success that others are slow to find.

But if you are one of those who has risen rapidly towards success, you may have a different perspective to throw on the fulfillment of desires. It is really an uncomfortable existence, as you see it. You have lost contact with other human beings, and you are not so sure about yourself. There seem to be some inhibitions in the area of love, some guilt about competition, some annoying physical conditions that cannot be organized away. You seem to be so good at managing others, but can you manage yourself?

To answer this question, let's consider the story of some successful graduate students who were in a group such as you may be a part of today. They were campus leaders, big men among a collection of less talented individuals in a professional seminar on personal development.

The successful students were intellectually aware of their needs for understanding and compassion. They heaped words upon words of explanation, but nothing was happening inside. They still could not see any personal possibility of failure. When other students pointed to their lack of humanity, the adequate ones were most distressed. Here was an area of life in which they could not will competence. They would have to learn from others.

As the meeting progressed, the leaders admitted their disenchantment with the rewards they had received. Like the brighter students in other professions, they rejected the provincialism and organizational emphasis that were the basis for many rewards they had received. Recognition by the home church or leading pastors did not seem significant to them.

The rejection of conventional success standards was heightened by the experience of two students as they came into close contact with ministers. In their home and college churches, the young men were either emotionally ignored or ecclesiastically exploited. In high school they were sent out as evangelists. No training was offered or supervision provided. They were expected to "make good" on the basis of personal talent and piety. One of the students had been handled in a different way. His pastor had given him tasks that were consistent with his age and had shown a personal interest in his development of tasks in the church and community. There was no expectation that he could do a great deal more than others of his age.

As a result of high school and college contacts with professionals in their field, the successful students determined to be more warm and friendly than the ministers whom they had encountered. Since they had opportunity on the weekend for part-time pastoral work, they tried to be personally interested in the people whom they served. But despite their zeal, there still was emotional inhibition. They were still racing for success. The more provincial goals had been discarded, but other rewards had taken their place. Grades, academic honors, and scholarly recognition were now of great importance.

Zeal for academic approval consumed the time and interest which they might have given to their attractive and devoted wives. Two of the women had accepted neglect for some time. In fact, they had been very successful in their own college and church work and in sharing the standards of their husbands who were "succeeding." One of the wives did voice her complaints at the insensitivity of her husband and was instrumental in leading him to a warmer and more open relationship with many people. During the process, both of them freely confessed their own immaturity and their desire to grow up together.

The Struggle to Surrender

Awareness of some of their characteristics did not stop the students' race for success. But it did sensitize them to signs of emotional distress which came during a second course on the psychology of religion. At the beginning of this second course, the most cautious of the successful students was concerned about his lack of feeling for people. He sought counsel on the ways by which he could be received as a warm and interested person by his peers. A second student developed acute gastritis. After his medical examination he said, "This is the price you pay for racing to success. I had better stop this rat race, or I will have an ulcer." The remaining student went into a week-long depression, precipitated by the dawning awareness of his indifference to his bride, and the acknowledgment of an overwhelming work load.

This was not the first time that each of these men had developed similar symptoms. The difference was in their interpretation of what was happening. In college they had soon returned to their former feverish pace. This time they paused to examine themselves.

The key struggle was to drop their idol of perfectionism.

This involved the acceptance of some personal limitations and the sharpening of their personal identity. Two of the students decided that they knew enough about church work and were happy enough with the pastoral relationships to turn more completely toward their academic studies. Over a period of a month they sought the best way to tell their church that they wished to resign. Both were highly gratified by the response of the laymen when they discussed with deacons or with the total congregation the awareness of their limitations and the determination which they now had to be more humble and honest in their commitments. Three months later these students referred to their resignation from the church as a breakthrough in the development of feelings toward people whom they had served. The third student was confronted with an opportunity to assume additional academic responsibilities which would have been a sign of faculty approval. The student declined this invitation in order that he might devote himself more strictly to study and personal development.

The surrender of certain activities was accompanied by a release of affection. Before the students resigned their extra activities, they experienced deep guilt for having attempted to do so much in a superficial way. Most of all, they were oppressed by their casual treatment of a wife or a classmate. As one of the students said: "Now I can really love my wife because I realize how much I need her. She has loved me despite my unwillingness to love her." When another student was asked if his wife resented the drop in income, he said: "No, we talked about it, and she says that she feels more like continuing work since we can have the weekends to ourselves."

Deliverance from compulsive self-idealization was accompanied by openness in personal discussion with fellow students. Peers began to inquire as to the reasons for the successful student's limitation of activity. The successful men told what had happened to them when they were asked.

Other students, who were on top academically, shared the three students' intellectual rejection of denominational success standards. But some of these students could not accept the emotional content of a decision to limit activities that brought approval. The successful students were most often rejected by those who shared the characteristics of high academic performance, student approval, emotional inhibition, and isolation.

The successful students were now beginning to question the unspoken assumptions of their denominational background. They had begun to see unceasing activity as a sign of pride or an unwillingness to accept adult limitations of strength and interest. A desire to serve remained, but it was now becoming a means of glorifying God rather than an end in itself. The students also broke with the twentieth century religious emphasis upon mighty acts of men who make no confession of their failures or alarms. One of the students phrased his new awareness of humility in a chapel prayer:

> O Father, lead us just now out of the noise and rush of our days into the quiet rest of worship. Give up the courage to look deep within ourselves and the good sense to confess the sins we see. Forgive us, merciful Father, for foolhardy attempts to rule our own lives, when Jesus Christ alone is Lord; for the deadening familiarity with which we take the

Gospel; for having no time for sympathy and understanding with our fellow students and families; for not having cared for the man in the ditch; for trying so impersonally to add a whit to our status; for failing to redeem the time we spend in learning; for having been so poor stewards of our energies that they are spread too thin and stretched too tight; for seeing the mote and blindly missing the beam: for our casual prayers and perfunctory worship.

As we have been judged by thy holiness, so may we be forgiven by thy love. For we take courage in thy mercy and do not wish to presume upon it. Only show us clearly that we now must go and declare it to those yet unforgiven.

We wait, our Father, the moving of thy spirit to create among us the miracle of true fellowship. For we openly admit our need of communion with Thee and with each other. Reconcile us to Thee, so that we shall be able to be reconciled to our brothers. As we have been set in saving relationships with Thy Son and our friends, we ask now to be preserved therein. Help us to mirror thy mercy in all our dealings with mankind.

And for the learning pilgrimage to which we have been called, we earnestly desire to hear the inward testimony of the Holy Spirit to the truth we need to know. Instruct us in the right division of thy Word and in the manner of life a minister should lead. For we lack knowledge, and we ask of Thee. Teach us discipline and perseverance for our toil, and save us from unnecessary fatigue.

Now, O Father, make us ready to hear the message appointed to this hour. Move within it and among us, Holy Spirit, so that it shall become thy Word to us. Undergird him who seeks to declare thy Word and make us who hear sensitive to receive it.

And having heard, may we never stray from Thee, who are the way; or disbelieve Thee, who are the truth; or die without Thee, who art the life—even Christ Jesus our Lord. Amen.

The Return of Spirituality

The prayer was one sign of deepening spiritual life of the successful students. They often spoke of their confrontation with adolescent and denominational success standards as a new conversion experience.

In group discussion the students said that they had moved from a childhood state of religious feeling to a college inhibition of feeling and now to a return of faith during their seminary career. They described their spiritual pilgrimage as follows.

In childhood the students felt many emotions about God. Two of the men were not from formally religious homes. However, one of them remembered the day when he looked at a burning trash pile and thought, "Well, I know that I will not burn in hell like that because I did some things yesterday for a little kid." Another recalled his weeping at the thought of hell. But he was consoled by the thought that God would make him successful if he would just do his bidding. The service of God was the same as the perfection of himself. The third student felt no "fear of God" in childhood, but in church groups he was constantly reminded of his "influence." He said: "Neither of my parents objected to my dancing; my mother even encouraged it. I did not dance in high school or even in college because my pastor and others at *church* had drilled into me the notion that participation in dancing would 'hurt my witness' as Christian. I was proud of the fact I refused to dance even though my mother encouraged it."

By middle or late adolescence, the students were swept with strong religious emotions. The first student was moved to tears at the thought that God loved him even though he had not done all that his Creator had required. The second student was zealous to do whatever he could to prove himself successful in high school as a Christian. For all three students there were pervasive feelings that God would reward those who worked diligently for him. In the southwestern culture there were many rewards in this world for those who served the church.

These rewards came immediately to the successful students in college. They were youth evangelists and/or academic favorites. Intellectual development and church activities dominated their lives. They experienced no conspicuous failure, although they often felt that they had missed out either as the natural result of their Christian service or the wise use of God-given talents. Two of them courted and married young women who shared their standards and had achieved on campus. The third married the queen of a state beauty contest after he graduated from college. He was very impressed by her character and intellect, which won her college recognitions.

The confrontation of student group evaluations led these men to long for the joy and assurance of religious feelings which they had in adolescence. But they wanted the religious experience to be more mature. In the past, adolescent religion had provided them assurance so long as they asked no questions. The door to success had been opened as they fulfilled all the requirements of those who would give approval. These men felt that they did not serve God unless they were continually busy. Spirituality had been service conceived of as activity.

The Confirmation of Identity

At the deepest—or highest—level there is the challenge of confirmation before God. Could these men stand before God with the knowledge they now have of themselves? One of the men faced the issue in a senior clinical training course. He had accepted a *quantitative* limitation of his activities, but could accept no diminution of the quality of his work. He became depressed because he was not functioning at a "high professional level" as a student chaplain. Intense hostility developed toward his theological supervisor. In a supervisory conference, the student recognized that hostility toward a theological authority was an expression of a hidden hostility toward God. His supervisor replied that the student resented God because God was perfect and he could find nothing wrong with him. The student reported: "A wave of uncontrollable feeling swept over me as I experienced the gracious presence of a God who could accept my hostile feelings toward him. In the most personal and magnificent way I became aware of the meaning of the crucifixion. It had never occurred to me—in a deeply personal way—that God could accept my hostility." This student could receive the full impact of religious feeling again. When he admitted some of his failures before God and man, he found acceptance on a deeper level from both.

chapter 6
can i make disclosures with composure?

The last chapter closed with the testimony of an "uncontrollable feeling" sweeping over a student. That sounds dangerous to some of us. We fear any lack of control, especially before other people, and "uncontrollable feeling" means so many different things. To one of us, it would be no more than blushing or a watering of the eyes. Another person might imagine a full breakdown in hysterical crying or psychotic rage. In any group experience where people are being asked to talk about themselves, we face the questions: Will I be able to really say how I feel without embarrassing myself? Will I go too far, cause others to be uncomfortable, feel like a fool when the session is over?

A Time to Speak

We can summarize all these questions by asking what is fitting under specific circumstances. That question leads us back to the assumptions and practices of our family up to this time. Within the family we have learned what to say about ourselves, when, and where.

Some of us cannot even get to this question. We don't believe that anything should be disclosed at any time, anywhere. A talk about ourselves is associated with painful memories from the past. If you feel this way, you might need some initial conversations with one counselor before you enter a group experience.

Larry Babbs was one of those quiet men who would nod his head in a group and say nothing. When I saw him for individual counsel, he gradually unfolded the story of searing childhood memories. His father always seemed to be ill-tempered. The son attributed this to the harsh conditions of the father's work, but in addition, the father would come in drunk on the weekend. He would abuse his wife and beat the children. "Many times I wanted to say something, but I knew it would just make things worse," said Larry. "He really had a bad temper and would have beat us worse if we had stood up to him. When he would yell at my mother or put her down, I could not help but watch. There was nothing I could do. I would tell myself 'yes, he will get it someday, yes he will,' but not from me. I could see, but yet not see."

Larry is very sensitive to what is going on around him, yet he pretends that he sees nothing. At least he gives no response. He seemed to appreciate the individual counseling sessions that were offered to him, but he did not go into any group. On one occasion he said that the best life for him was at home in his own room, with a job that would bring in a little money for his mother and himself. He was happy with the thought that he might give her some support in her old age. His father was now dead, and no one would menace him when he showed affection for his mother.

Larry has made an adjustment to life by returning to an earlier stage of development. He is now satisfied to do the kinds of things that he wanted so much to do for one whom he loved when he was a child. He does not tell his mother what he is thinking about, but he is able to show her how he feels by little acts of devotion.

Isn't this enough for most people? Why not remain silent about our own suffering or that of others? To answer that question, we need to know that Larry first came for counsel because his marriage was breaking up. He said that his wife was always "putting him down." She said that he had no initiative, that she hardly knew him. Larry explained that he was doing the best that he could. If a job did not turn out right, he withdrew without making a fuss. He was never advanced in any position and was usually the first to be fired. When his wife complained about this and other matters, Larry would sit in the living room, rocking and humming. So far as the wife was able to tell, he had hardly heard what she said.

Larry could not understand his wife's frustration and was bewildered when she left him to live with another man. He said: "I never fussed at her or gave her any trouble. She had no cause to say those bad things about me. I tried to do the best that I could." Larry was repeating in adult life the pattern of childhood. He withdrew into himself during periods of disappointment and was unwilling to disclose anything about himself.

If you assume, like Larry, that no disclosure is necessary, then you cannot move very far in life. You may make an adjustment in the protected world of mother or father, grandmother or grandfather, but you will be a continual source of frustration to husband or wife, son or daughter. You will have few friends, because people complain that they do not know you.

We have to give a part of ourselves if we are going to receive anything from others. The motto is "Live and

Give." This is especially true in modern youth culture, where the keys to acceptance are attitudes like awareness, authenticity, sharing, and openness. We are challenged to show our real self, to let people know that we are aware of our immediate feelings and can articulate them.

If we are going to be accepted in any group outside of our parents, we will have to do some sharing. This is not strange to those who have grown up in a healthy family. In contrast to Larry, most of us have learned how to talk about ourselves at home. Dr. Sidney Jourard of the Department of Psychology at the University of Florida found that many young adults had shared a good deal with their parents and vice versa. There was no generation gap between parents and children who were warmly together in solving problems. In his interviews with young adults, Dr. Jourard found that the young wives had done the most talking, usually with their mothers. This does not seem to be an indictment of sons and fathers, since the men in his study generally did not talk as much about themselves as women under any circumstances.

Young adults who had shared themselves at home were quite willing to disclose who they were with a marital partner. The women in the study seemed to know more and tell more about themselves both before and in marriage. The men were more reluctant to speak about themselves before marriage and more willing to share their feelings after marriage. The bond of marriage is a generator of intimacy.

Both men and women reported close friends with whom they shared a good deal as they were growing up. These peer relationships added a good deal to the comfortable feeling of young adults in talking about themselves with others in a group.

The conclusion of Dr. Jourard was that no man can come to know himself except as an outcome of disclosing himself to other people. A person who has been able to make himself known to others will learn by this what kind of person he is both as he speaks of himself and as others react to him. The research showed that we are mostly able to talk about ourselves with those who are like us. We share our values with those who would seem to be accepting and understanding. And we speak most intimately with those who love us.

What does this research mean for a group interaction? First, we can conclude that there is little need for a group experience among adults who grew up in a family where there was open communication, who had close friends in childhood with whom they shared themselves, and who are happily married to a mate who can speak and show what both of them feel. Sensitivity or therapy sessions are most often sought by persons who have a defect in one of those areas: family, friends, marriage partner. When something is lacking in those communications, then it must be made up in a more general setting.

But how are we to catch up with the conversations that were denied us in earlier years? How can we learn to talk now with those who seem cold to us? An answer to these questions is a second conclusion from the research of Dr. Jourard. We can speak in a group as we would have spoken in the family or with close friends in the past, if they could have permitted this. Since that experience was denied us, we can now recreate happier and more satisfying circumstances in this substitute family. We speak to another person in this group as though he could have been a close friend in the past or unfold some of the sentiments that we would have liked to speak as a child to mother or father.

These conditions will be possible if others agree with us to tell about themselves and to show attention when we talk about ourselves. If we all know that we are trying to catch up on some parts of life that were missing from the past, then our disclosure will not seem to be extreme or odd.

When the group understands that all of us are trying to catch up with life in some way, then our conversations as a child with father or a little girl with a close friend will not seem strange. There is a mutual pact of understanding. Each person has a right in this group to recreate in the rest of us a substitute family, a temporary friend, a mate for the evening. We can see by the lives of others that something has been missed, and this is our chance to fill in some ground that was lost in the past.

Why would we have to do this in the artificial surroundings of a group? Why shouldn't this be done in the home or with those for whom we care? Certainly the goal of a group experience is to create the understanding and conditions that will lead to warm and intimate sharing in family and among friends, but here we can draw a third lesson from the experience of adults. We cannot "lift ourselves up by our bootstraps" in the field of communication. If we have not had adequate models of sharing in the past, we certainly cannot create them out of our own thin imagination today. We need to be with people who are working on this task with us, and this should include at least one person who has the skill to show and tell what we are looking for.

Furthermore, a person who has never disclosed himself with any composure will be self-defeating. He will either go too far and embarrass himself or others, or he will cut off the attempts which he makes to tell about himself or attempts of others to move closer toward him. Despite our desire to be open in communication, we often "hang up" on another person before any of us have really begun to talk.

Our communication cutoffs are often revealed when we describe failures in decision-making. Couples often come into groups for just that reason. They have had so many fights about decisions that they know something is wrong. "Why can't we make decisions like ordinary people and get along?"

In a family therapy session, Barbara brought up this question before her parents did. An alert thirteen-year-old, she said, "Well, our family cannot really decide to do anything. Daddy will say that he is tired, and Mamma will say that we should go to a movie. She may fuss a little, and he will say nothing. On Saturday I will propose a picnic, and Mamma will say that we must buy groceries. Daddy says that he wants to play golf. We just stew around, and nothing is done."

FATHER: "Well, doctor, she is right. We never can make a decision. Like last Friday when we left here. Barbara wanted to go to a movie, and Janice (Mother) wanted to go out for a nice dinner."

MOTHER: "So we ended up eating a hamburger, and the movie wasn't any good."

BARBARA: "But Mamma, it was the movie that you said that you wanted to go to."

FATHER: "Well, anyway, I tried to say then that we could not go to both things the same night. It was already 7:00 and the movie was going to be at 8:00. I couldn't think of any nice restaurant that we could go to and get good service within one hour."

MOTHER: (turning to counselor) "You would think that a man who has been in business in this town for five years would know where the best restaurants are. He certainly eats out enough in the evening with his friends!"

FATHER: (smiles weakly) "Well, anyway, there was not enough time."

COUNSELOR: "Is there time for the two of you to go out to a dinner on occasion?"

MOTHER: "He never seems to find the time. I don't want to complain about him, because he is a good husband and is very attentive to me and the children when he is at home, but his business seems to keep him out so many evenings each week. I wish we could agree on a time when we would go out each week."

FATHER: "But if we did agree, Janice would still complain about something. She would think that the service was not good or that the food was not right or else we go too late and can't get into the place we want to get into."

MOTHER: "Well, if we would just go more often, it wouldn't be such a problem, but when you only get to go out once every couple of months, you really get your heart set on the very best that one time."

COUNSELOR: "I gather that you, Janice, would like to go out to eat at least once a week. Have the three of you talked about this?"

FATHER: "No, we never seem to have time for a discussion."

MOTHER: "Oh, yes, we talked about this some months ago, but we never made a decision."

BARBARA: "Well, I would keep Tom and Billy when you want to go."

COUNSELOR: "So our problem now is to decide on how often you will go and where you will go."

FATHER: "But I don't know if I could pick a place that would please her."

MOTHER: "Well, when you get to go only once every couple of months, you want to go to some place where you really can enjoy yourself once in a while."

FATHER: "All right, let's set up a schedule and look at our calendars [he notices that Janice turns away from him and looks up at the ceiling]. Well, I guess this is the way it often goes, Doctor. I try to manage things at home like I do at the office [smiles]. Here is the big businessman who is going to manage the family like he does a corporation."

COUNSELOR: "And you show your resentment, don't you Janice?"

MOTHER: "I don't know. It just seems that he should be able to find the time for us to do some things together, but he never seems to pick the right places."

COUNSELOR: "Well, I see that you are defeating each other. Hugh, you do seem to know why you are annoying your wife when a decision is to be made. If you can be less formal and talk straight across to your wife, she may be able to hear you better. Janice, you don't think right now about the way in which you cut Hugh down as he tries to work with you."

FATHER: "Yes, I think that we have to work on these things together."

MOTHER: "You think I should do less complaining about the decisions?"

COUNSELOR: "Yes. Decision-making is a bargaining process. If he will give up some of his office routine and dinners with clients to enjoy an evening with you, then you have to give up something in return."

MOTHER: "Well, I don't know what I would be giving up. It seems as though I would be getting everything."

COUNSELOR: "Not quite. You would have to give up fussing if the evening were not perfect."

MOTHER: "Well, what I want is an evening out like we used to have before we were married. He made all the arrangements then and chose the best places, and we had a wonderful time."

FATHER: "But when I am running all day long, I don't think about making the arrangements. It seems to me that we could agree on the time and the place and you could make some calls about the arrangements [Janice looks up again at the ceiling]."

COUNSELOR: "Well, Janice, you have cut him off again. Do you know why? [She shakes her head.] When he asked you to cooperate with him as an adult, you put your nose up in the air. You want him to still treat you as a young bride or as a young girl. You expect him to make all of the arrangements like a big man of the world who is taking care of a little girl. The part of the bargain that you will have to keep is to act like an adult who takes some responsibility for the arrangements, and also takes some responsibility for her feelings when she is out with her husband for an evening. In short, you will have to give up acting like a little girl who is disappointed if everything is not perfect. Have I insulted you by saying this?"

MOTHER: "Well, I do go to pieces if things don't turn out right. That's one reason that we have come to see you. I don't even know where we would go to dinner. What would you suggest?"

COUNSELOR: "I would suggest that the two of you make the following decisions before you see me next week. First, how often will you go out together? Second, pick out the place. Third, decide who is going to make the arrangements by calling ahead and setting the time."

FATHER: "Well, we'll try, but it never has worked out before."

COUNSELOR: "It won't work this time, either, unless the two of you are aware of the way in which you keep from making decisions."

FATHER: "You mean like my businessman attitude?"

COUNSELOR: "Yes, and the way that Janice cuts you off and has her own set of demands."

Barbara has disclosed some problems between mother and father that the mother is reluctant to look into. Hugh has more awareness of how he cuts off a decision by the role that he assumes. Janice is not quite ready to confess that she is a delayed adolescent who expects everything to be just right, or it is totally wrong.

In the next interview, the couple made a summary statement that illustrates the point of this lesson. Both said: "You are trying to get us to state our *expectations* of each other." I agreed. Then we talked more about each of them. Janice expected a marriage in which she would be cared for and to some extent coddled. Hugh was expecting to be a very adequate gentleman who would make much money and many decisions in the world and would therefore be treated with respect in his home, and his wife would be happy. I discussed these expectations with each, but neither of them had discussed these expectations with each other. As a result, they had just acted as though the other one knew what was required. As a result, they were in constant conflict, for his decisions in the family were less than perfect, and her expectations exceeded perfection. Until these people could begin to disclose something of themselves to each other, they would not be satisfied by any decisions that were made.

Both Hugh and Janice would like to make decisions together, but neither has been aware of the way in which each cuts off the other in communication. A third party is necessary for them to disclose themselves to each other without creating additional problems. The "additional problems" might be a violent argument or a long period of sulking. Both of these are avoided by the intervention of some knowledgeable person who can describe what is happening to people while their emotions are being blocked or released. With this kind of control, a couple can loosen up while retaining their composure.

A teaching leader will be most helpful in saving a person's face as he tells about himself. The leader does this by explaining behaviors and giving meaning to statements for the entire group. He increases self-understanding and awarness through a summary of how this word or gesture has general significance. That is, all members of the group can learn something from what has happened to this individual. If Janice and Hugh had been in a larger group, a leader could have asked how Janice's look toward the ceiling was going to cut off communications with Hugh. When members of the group had identified this sign and its meaning, the leader might ask if others could give examples of signs that cut off communication between them and other people. Janice would not feel that she was the only one who showed nonverbal disgust. Other people did the same thing in their own way.

Group Teaching

A sensitive group is like an accordion. People can close in on us to be sure we admit something which others see in us and we have denied. Or the group may open up, expand with our feelings, and be a regular cheering session for the enthusiastic insights that we have experienced.

Either of these movements will aid our disclosure with composure. If a leader or another member is moving in on one of our half-buried resentments, we will not have to face our accuser alone. There are others in the group who will either rephrase his observations in another way or perhaps disagree with what he has said. In fact, one of the major problems in group management is to keep a self-styled rescuer from taking an alert person off of our back before we have really seen what he is trying to tell us. In a well-managed group, the leader or another member will call attention to this diversion and return the discussion to our problem.

Carlos was angry with the grade he had received in a graduate seminar. In the group discussion lab for graduate students, he said:

CARLOS: "I think that some of our professors are hard of hearing, and some of them are downright threatened by what we know. I don't see where all of this psychoanalysis is going to help me in business, but that assistant professor in psychology said that I was insensitive to the needs of others. He said that my analysis of the management problems would just push people away from me. Well, I don't think that I am any more pushy than anybody else who wants to get ahead in his work!"

ARCHIE: "Well, I noticed that in our sessions here you break right in and say what you want to, no matter who is—"

CARLOS: "Who do these professors think they are, anyway? If they want to grade me on my ability or my performance, that's okay. But when they start talking about what kind of a person I am and how I get along with other people, I think that is going too far. I think we should organize some kind of a protest about this. We have our rights."

LEADER: "And what kind of rights does Archie have?"

CARLOS: "That's what I mean. All students have rights against you professors. You're a good guy, Vic, but I know you have to be on the side of the administration. You wouldn't like what I'm saying."

MARY: "And I don't like what you are saying. We don't need somebody from the psychology department to tell us that you are pushy. You run over people right here in this group every week."

CARLOS: "Who? When? Just give me an example."

MARY: "Well, Archie, how do you feel about what Carlos did to you?"

CARLOS: "I haven't done anything to Archie. What are you talking about?"

LEADER: "How about looking at Archie when you say that."

CARLOS: "Sure I'll look at him [turning]. All right, Archie, what do you have to say to me?"

ARCHIE: "That you cut me off in the midst of a sentence. You had a big speech prepared, and nobody else counted. You don't even know that you did it."

CARLOS: [looks surprised] "Did what? I was just trying to talk about the way things are around here before Vick tried to smother it all up."

MARY: "We want to talk about the way that you try to smother us."

CARLOS: "Like when? Suppose you give me an example?"

MARY: "I just did, and you turned on Archie like you were the district attorney and were ready to tear him to pieces. I don't think that you even know when you were doing this. At least you did not know when you were interrupting Archie or turning on him with such force."

CARLOS: "Why should all of you be with the professors?"

ARCHIE: "If you will permit me to say something, it is my opinion that we are not with the professors as much as we are glad to hear that somebody had the power to put you down. At least I'm glad to hear it. It's about time. If I may make a little speech, I would say that you are going to careen around life until somebody busts you real good, and then you'll wake up surprised and wonder what has happened."

LEADER: "Hasn't a little of that just occurred here?"

CARLOS: "Yeah, yeah. It sure looks like everybody wants to bust me good."

The conversation continued for half an hour. Carlos went out of the seminar, shaking his head and saying, "I never thought that you people felt this way about me. I just don't get it." But fellow students observed that Carlos was a little more subdued for the next week and would seek out one or two trusted associates to ask them if it were really true that he didn't listen to other people. He would not hear what was said by one authority, but he was slowed down by a group effort.

A group also supports those who have begun to talk about themselves but fear that they are going to be disgraced by this. In one session, an older woman said that several people had talked about depression in the last few meetings. She thought that most of the people in the group were depressed at times, and she wondered if there were some general rule that they might learn about this experience. What had people learned about their own depression that would help others get through a trying time? After several people had spoken, a young housewife hesitantly remarked that she had finally accepted some physical relationship to her "blue spells." She said she knew. "I know that a lot of this is just me, but some of it is the tired feeling I have from being with the children all day—and when I have a cold or something like that, I know for sure that I am going to get down in the dumps. My husband and my doctor have told me about this, but I used to think that it was silly of me to let myself go that way. Well, now I am not so silly about that, at least. I mean, when I have a bad cold and the kids have the flu, I just let the house go and don't try to get out of bed and clean up everything." She stopped and looked about her. The older woman said, "Dear, that's something that I really need to hear. My doctor has told *me* that I should slow down, but I don't want to hear it. I go like a house afire for weeks, and then I end up like you saw me last week. I should have learned a lesson when I was your age."

The younger woman managed a wan smile and sat contentedly through the rest of the session. She had nothing more to say, but her relaxed posture and attention to the remarks of others were signs that she felt that she was a part of the group. She had made a contribution, and it had been of value to an older person.

The Dangers of Disclosure

A healthy person sets limits on what he says to others. The young woman in the previous example did not describe everything about her relationships with her husband. She told that which was necessary to help herself and the group at this time. It is only in a carefully structured group for unhealthy persons that each one is to give complete details about himself and those who are close to him as the group meets from week to week for two or three years.

One of the dangers of disclosure is that a person will confuse a group experience with normal people and a therapy group for the long-term treatment of neurotic or psychotic disorders. This problem is usually clarified in the early meetings of either type of group. For example, a church group announced three sessions for "family enrichment" and sought to recruit regular church attenders from throughout the city for these sessions.

The forty-eight women and four men who attended the first meeting were mostly suburbanites with time to attend afternoon teas, committees, or family enrichment seminars. When they had been divided into four "teams," each leader began his session with a question: "What is the most important reason for your attendance of these sessions?"

In one group, an attractive housewife sighed and said that she wanted "to feel like more than an expensive mistress for my husband. I want to really feel like a person. How can I be more of a person with him?" Others nodded affirmation and began to ask questions or make comment. Clearly the young lady had struck a responsive chord in the hearts of other capable, mildly frustrated women.

But a middle-aged, heavyset woman was frowning during this group movement. She finally had her turn: "I don't see why the church doesn't do more for people who really need help. Jesus! We've got sick people around here. I could tell you some stories that would really bug you. You young things don't know anything. What's all this stuff about loving, anyway? If you had been in some of the places I've been in, you wouldn't talk about love." She sneered, shut her mouth in a tight line, and glared around the group.

After a tense silence, the leader said: "Now that we have gotten to know each other, let's see what topic we might begin with. What do you suggest?" Suggestions were made about "being more responsive," "showing warmth," "being understanding," "how to keep going when its rough." Again the resentful woman intimidated the young matrons: "How about some talk on people who are locked up for years and have all their rights taken away from them?

How about corrupt politicians and crooked police? What about some church people who don't care—including some preachers? *I'll* tell you about some things that will make you wonder why you ever give money to a church—"

"Since most of us have spoken," quickly said the leader, "I think we should establish some contract. What about the time when we arrive and depart?" He moved on rapidly through time setting to another question: "Will we all agree to be here every time, or what?" The heavy-set matron sat back, puffing on a cigarette while everyone else nodded that they would attend all three sessions. Then she spoke: "You can count me out. I don't think you really know what is going on. I've been hurt in some ways that you don't know about. You wouldn't understand. And robbed—"

The young women exchanged glances with each other and a few eyebrows were raised. Again the leader cut her off with: "Let's talk about this for a moment after we conclude our session, shall we?" (He nods at the woman, who stares back at him.)

The leader suppressed one member of the group who did not fit into a collection of mildly dissatisfied, but generally adequate people. As he suspected, the hostile woman had a story of chronic bitterness to tell him after the session. Her son had been mentally ill for many years. She had blamed everyone for this, including the pastor, county judge, and a variety of doctors. Her need was for a group of people with similar difficulties, who would not be intimidated by her references to "awful occurrences," as she put it. In the presence of those who had been through as much as she has, there would be more composure when she made her disclosures.

When everyone in a group has been through shattering experiences that produce conspicuous failures, personal disclosures are not only received with more understanding, but also with more confidence. There is a common bonding that prevents premature or indiscreet talk about the problems of group members with people in the family or community.

On the other hand, in a "growth group" for people who have the psychological or financial resources to conceal their intimate conflicts, there is much worry about secrecy. "Who will tell what we have shared?" is a question that soon must be discussed. There must not only be some group agreement, there must also be a belief among most in the group that all are capable of keeping their mouths shut outside the session. One group did not "get going" until an indiscriminate talker had been frozen out of the sessions. When I asked how this was done, one participant said: "I guess we just waited him out. If he asked a question, none of us answered. Some of us talked among ourselves about not saying anything much while he was still in the group. I guess the word got around, because he seemed to lose interest and stopped coming. Then things loosened up."

The group leader confirmed this opinion. She said: "It's a neighborhood church and people know each other—or want to. There's lots of interaction, dinners, fellowship, gathering in homes. They stay here. Its a settled community. So they don't talk to just anybody, and they know who the gossips are, so they keep quiet around them. This particular gossip did get bored—there was no payoff in the group, no juicy stories. So he just stopped coming."

The consequences of disclosure will depend on the continuing association of participants. In the neighborhood church group, quietness was maintained until all were sure of each other. They would be together in church, neighborhood, and family for a long time. But what if the occasion had been a weekend marathon in the mountains, with people collected from four states? The possibility of continued interaction would be greatly reduced, and the conversation might reach a deeper level in less time.

However, the press of time is another danger in disclosure. When a person does not have time to think through what he is about to say, he may be embarrassed and regretful. Sometimes his feelings get out of hand and he becomes a psychic casualty. He may "come apart" in the sessions or worse, he may return home and begin to cry, stay in his room, "tell off" his associates, talk for hours about his problems, decide to leave his wife. These are some of the risks of an anonymous meeting in which the leader has not screened applicants and can take no continued responsibility for those who, like Humpty Dumpty, cannot be put back together again on short notice.

A related difficulty is the attempt of novices to try "implosive" techniques. That is, individuals are encouraged in a group to "get in contact" with some of their most painful feelings: to cry about frustrations of childhood, express rage about frustrations in the family, "act crazy" if they have fears of becoming mentally ill. With no controls and experience, the sensitive person is exploited.

A less dangerous but annoying tendency of some sharing groups is the emphasis upon hostility. In the artificial surroundings of a therapeutic group, people are told "say exactly what you feel about another person." There are leading statements such as "Do you *really* like him?"

"This is a place where you can tell people off without retribution." Since some young adults have some hostilities toward those in competition with them and those who are holding them down, there usually is plenty of anger to be expressed. If this is a phase in the group process, it can be balanced with earlier or later expression of tenderness, love, forgiveness, and affection. But in some groups, feelings of hostility rate higher than any other sharing. Anger is considered to be the ultimate reality.

There are occasions when very deprived or depressed people must express long buried resentments. An expert therapist led a high school senior to tell her mother of her anger over the beating of younger family members. But along with the encouragement to speak critically there was also a question: "Can you as a young adult understand some of the reasons why your mother has acted as she does?" The goal of the sessions was not the expression of hostility for its own sake, but the resolution of conflict and reconciliation.

Some persons may be so thrilled with an encounter group that they do not recognize the artificiality of their surroundings. It is true that they have experienced themselves in a more authentic way during the weekend "marathon." There is acceptance and understanding in a sensitivity laboratory. But this is not the world to which they will return on Monday morning. There is a difference between the occasional sharing of deep feelings with a trusted and loved person versus the impulsive statement of hostility and rejection to a rigid employer or an unstable family member.

Therapeutic groups in community mental health centers usually try to move through the period of intimate sharing to a recognition of necessary controls in regular relationships. Therapists ask: "Now that you have experienced this feeling, how will you manage it during work?" One phase of therapy is an understanding of self and contact with personal emotion. Another phase is the integration of those feelings with the roles that a person plays in life. How do we communicate ourselves in ways that others will accept and respect?

Transparent or Translucent?

The communication of self-awareness should be in a spirit of love and self-control. The individual must not only know who he is, but how he perceives others and how they hear him. He must know in what ways he is like them and how he is different from them.

The awareness of similarities and differences will limit self-disclosure. We are to be as open with people as they will allow or can use for our mutual benefit. Selfhood sets boundaries.

An awareness of boundaries is a mark of respect for self and others. We do not tell everything that we know or think about an individual unless he is open to hear us. We do not listen to everything that another person would say about us. We hear that which is said with respect and at a time that it can be made a part of our self-image.

The filtering of communications is to be through a sensitive screen that we call socialization. Through years of training we have learned that communication is best through certain types of persons at specified times. On some occasions we are transparent about our feelings. At all times we are translucent. There are no barriers in transparency. This is the healthy condition of communication between intimate associates, parent and child, husband and wife. Whatever we are is to be known by them.

But we do not show everything that we feel to casual acquaintances, business associates, or professional coworkers. With them we are translucent. That is, our principles and our motives are evident. This is the steady light of a character that shines through all relationships. But the brief shadows of pain, the fleeting association of this person with another, do not show clearly. They are sublimated for the sake of our daily work or the appropriateness of an occasion. If another member of a panel discussion is the spitting image of an enemy, why reveal this disquieting thought? We can concentrate upon our common task in the discussion and may find in time that this particular person is interesting and friendly. We can keep our composure without having to make a full disclosure.

chapter 7
can i make a good decision?

The "Charlie Browns" of this world get the most out of a group experience. If you are one of those indecisive people, you may wonder how this can be true. Won't people laugh or sneer when your hesitant ways are revealed?

"Lucys" will yell at you, of course, but the Lucys also learn something from the group.

MR. RANTHROW: (in a couples' group) "For myself, I would like to find out how we can be happier people together. I mean, Grace and me. I think that we work very well together, but, uh, well that would be my contract for this group."

LEADER: "Well, it sounds a little vague. Maybe we can spell out the terms a little more specifically. What do you mean when you say that you don't get along?"

MR. RANTHROW: "Oh, nothing in particular. I just mean that when people respect each other they are much happier. Don't you think so?"

MRS. RANTHROW: "We are here because his mind is never easy with any decision and because I've yelled at him so much that our doctor said that we needed to do something or my nerves would be shot."

LEADER: "Could you give some typical illustration of what gets on your nerves?"

MRS. RANTHROW: "Well, like last night. Some man called from up in Connecticut and wanted him to stop by next Wednesday to talk about some property. George was out, so I told the man that he couldn't come until the following week. George had *told me* that he was going to be in Syracuse all week. Then when George came home, he frowned, then got on the phone and spent half an hour trying to find the man. Then he hemmed and hawed around. He made *me* look like a liar."

LEADER: "How's that?"

MRS. RANTHROW: "Well, he told that man that he *could* come up to Connecticut. I asked him why he couldn't make up his mind. I don't like to tell a person one thing and then find out something different the next minute."

MR. RANTHROW: (looks around and sees that the leader and other members of the group are looking at him) "Well, Grace, I tried to tell you that there was some flexibility in my schedule. I can make some adjustments—"

MRS. RANTHROW: (looking at the leader) "I told him that people would not respect him if he made commitments to them and then backed out on it. What will the people in Syracuse think about this?"

LEADER: "Are you acquainted with the people in Syracuse?"

MRS. RANTHROW: (slows down a bit) "Well, I met some of them at a party one time. I think that they are reliable people who should be treated right."

LEADER: "I wonder if you know why I asked you this particular question?"

MRS. RANTHROW: (shakes her head) "No. It just seems to me that anybody would know what to do in a situation like this and would do the right thing."

LEADER: "Mr. Ranthrow, would you or some other member of the group have an idea about this question that I asked?"

MR. RANTHROW: "Well, uh, uh, perhaps you are wondering how well she knows the business. (leader nods) I am often helped by her opinions, but she stays very close to home."

Mrs. Ranthrow was looking around the group. She was puzzled by the grin that appeared on one or two faces. At first she thought that they might be laughing at her husband, but then she had the uneasy feeling that they were amused at her.

MRS. TEDD: (who had been grinning the most) "This is just like my family. Mamma always knew *everything*. It's really funny when you see it in somebody else."

LEADER: "I'm sure that it was not very funny for you when you were younger, and I doubt that Mr. and Mrs. Ranthrow are having much fun out of the situation right now." (The couple stared at the leader with some sense of relief that he understood their situation.)

In this interchange, Mrs. Ranthrow has put Mr. Ranthrow down, as usual, but when people in the group noticed this, she comes down a notch herself.

Neither of these people was abandoned after the group knew of their typical way of relating. Instead, a controversy over decision-making was a topic of conversation on more than one occasion during the twelve sessions of this particular group. During those sessions, the group considered some typical questions that help "Lucy" and "Charlie Brown" to be more comfortable with the decisions that they make.

Who Am I?

The group is already getting to know Mr. and Mrs. Ranthrow. In time they can pass on some of their knowledge to this feuding couple. If they can accept it, decisions in the family will be more realistic. Mrs. Ranthrow may begin to see that her husband is not *always* confused and indecisive. He does know a few things and can make decisions in areas where she doesn't have much information. She may even see that it is not necessary for her to know everything all the time and to give directions without ceasing. As she reported in a later session, she was making some conscious effort to ask her husband what he had decided about some issues.

The group response must have been significant, for Mr. Ranthrow remembered that evening for years. During a chance meeting wtih the leader in another city, he said, "You remember those sessions that year? Well, I can still see the grin on that young girl's face. She really saw through my wife and me. I suddenly realized that other people understood. I would not have to defend myself all the time. I can't tell you what a relief it was. Grace wasn't so great a problem after that."

Mr. Ranthrow was no longer a worm. In the discussions he had gradually learned that people could have confidence in him and that it was realistic for him to assert himself on occasion. He might even say, in a nice way, "Grace, please get the telephone number of people who call me and let me respond to them. Sometimes I can work things out about engagements."

What Do I Live For?

Mr. and Mrs. Ranthrow know more of how they relate to each other, but how much do they really know about themselves? This brings us to the second question that makes a decision "good," or "bad." It is "What do I live for?" Our values will determine whether we have made up our minds in the right or wrong way, so far as we are concerned. These basic values in life will shape our sending and receiving of messages in a group. We hear people according to what is important to us, and we respond to them in accordance with our mission in the world, our desire to be worthwhile.

In the case of Grace Ranthrow, her mission in life was to know what is right and to do it. At least that is the way that she formulated the answer in a group session. Mrs. Tedd saw it a little differently. She said: "Grace, you seem to assume that you always know what is right. I'm not so sure. I mean, I'm not sure for myself, and I certainly do not think that you always know what is best for me."

MRS. RANTHROW (interrupting) "Now, dear, I didn't mean to say that I knew what was best for you to do. I just mean that I was always taught the meaning of right and wrong, and I expect to do that for myself."

MRS. TEDD: "But you keep *telling* the rest of us what to do, just like you do George. You don't seem to think that the rest of us can make any decisions for ourselves. Or at least you try to help us to be sure that we make the right decision as you see it. Well, that turns me off. I didn't go for that with my mother, and I don't take that from anybody else very well."

LEADER: In some ways, Grace reminds you of a know-it-all mother, (Miss Tedd nods) and Grace, you seem anxious to play the part of mother for everyone, beginning with George.

MRS. RANTHROW: "Well, that is certainly not my intention, but I do believe that some things need to be set straight sometime. I guess that I am a little overanxious about things. I do get a little too worried about things being just right. Maybe I say too much. But my mother always told me to speak up for what was right."

LEADER: "Since you have been taught things that you believe to be right, your mission in life seems to be setting other people straight as well. (pause) I'm not saying this just right. I don't mean to be putting you down. Maybe I have some problem with domineering women (grins)."

MR. RANTHROW: (group laughs) "I don't feel bad, I am often at a loss for words, too (more laughter). I think that Grace does mean well, but she does seem to be overly concerned about telling people what to do. You know she was a school teacher for many years, and—"

MRS. RANTHROW: "Oh, no, that has nothing to do with it."

So far, Mrs. Ranthrow isn't seeing very much about her mission in life. She has a blind faith that right is right and that she is the one who can tell people right from wrong. At times she may be "right," but she lacks self-awareness and control. The group would be relieved if she could just say: "My mission in life is to be the self-righteous matron of everyone in this room."

Other people are not so certain of what they live for. These are often the ones who receive the most help through a group consultation. A housewife may ask: "Is there any *real* reason for me to get up and get started every morning?" A retired and widowed businessman may ask: "Why do I spend this money going to Florida every winter, when I don't see anyone that I can help?" Others may say that they have never felt worthy, that their ideals have been defeated, that nothing ever seems to really turn out right for them.

Are you saying some of these things? If so, you will be surprised at the way that a group seems to nod, encourage, and support your groping toward some purpose in life. This is one of those universal searches in which all of us are sympathetic with others. We are not going the same way, our resources are different and our luck is varied, but we all seem to receive some strength from talking together about the age-old question "Quo Vadis?" Where are you going?

How Are Others Involved?

Some groups spend much time on goals but never seem to get anywhere. At least this was the conclusion of one research study. Psychologists found that comfortably-situated housewives were staying in group therapy for one or two years in a well-endowed mental health center. The women complained about the burden of their children, the inattentiveness of the husband, the lack of any real sense of meaning in life.

In contrast, women who entered group therapy in a nearby state hospital were seldom in a group for more than three months. The difference in time seemed to be a function of the group expectations. Very little was expected in the first group. In the second, the leader and group members talked often about responsibilities for their children, the need to understand and care for their husbands, the necessity of a quick return to their place in the community. The women in the second group probably had fewer psychological resources than the women in the first group, but they did more with what they had.

In answer to the question "What do I live for?" the people in the second group were saying: "I am spending a large part of my life for others." They were continually asking how others were involved in their feelings and decisions. What they said in this meeting had meaning beyond themselves.

In group or individual conversations, we can usually classify our decisions around one of three life-styles. The first is drifting. Like the housewives who met to complain about everything, we can move on with the stream of life, discontented and detached.

There usually are good reasons for the detachment. At least it seems that persons could justify their immobility. One young man came out of some group sessions with this comment: "My, they really told some terrible things about their background. Some of those people have been treated just awful. I don't see how they keep going at all. Of course, some of them don't. They have been beat right down into the ground."

But although this young man had some difficult experiences to relate, he didn't use these as an excuse for drifting. He found new strength and began to move out on his own. As John Bunyan said in *Pilgrim's Progress,* most of us fall into a slough of despond at some time. The essential question is, where do we climb out? "Faint heart" slogged back into the city of destruction. The "pilgrim" pushed his way out of the mud onto high ground. He was on his way to a celestial city.

Sometimes we are not quite sure as to where we are going. If we conceal our motives, we are self-deceived in decisions. This is a second style of life, concealment. Like Mrs. Ranthrow, we cannot really admit our basic motivation. She might not know how dominant she is. With such righteous reasoning, she may never look very closely into herself.

A group can be very valuable in questioning these rationalizations. We may continue to conceal, but at least we know that everyone is not convinced of our explanations. One purpose of the group experience is to move beyond concealment to honest confession. There may be much "confronting," but the purpose of telling each other what we see is to help each one to know just where he is moving in life, and why. Other people are involved in our decisions. If we know how they are involved, our acts will be more realistic and probably more convincing.

A third style of life is open awareness and confession. We try to know who we are and how we relate to others. If we hurt them, we honestly admit this and say that we are sorry. If we can make a change, we do so, for their benefit, and for ours. It is usually a little easier for the "Charlie Browns" to say this than it is for the "Lucys" to make confessions, but the Charlie Browns may be saying this to gain favor and not because he really understands himself and others. When he can move decisively on behalf of others, then we know that he is a committed person.

When and How Do I Act?

Mr. Ranthrow learned that when he was under attack from a dominant person, he began to stutter and retreat. This confirmed the opinion of Grace and others about him—he really didn't know what was going on. Actually, Mr. Ranthrow often knew more than it appeared, but he didn't show it. His big question in a group session was, "How do I know *when* I should say something?" He often had a good idea, but he was not sure of the timing and setting. The group experience was valuable to him as practice for self-affirmation in the world and at home. As he became less defensive, he was more aware of the appropriate time for a remark. He saw opportunities for remarks that would help others and sometimes made them. When he was congratulated for this, he would shyly smile. In time, he would even admit that he was of some help to his wife because he was more sensitive than she was to the appropriate opportunity for some remark. He never told her that she blundered into situations, but he did let her know that he was able to see some things that she did not. He attributed this to his sense of insecurity. She quickly pounced on that and did not recognize that her insensitivity also arose from insecurity. When she did not know what to do, she acted, which was a good deal of the time. With one or two shibboleths about life, she steered a strict course through all obstacles.

Mr. Ranthrow was more aware of the obstacles and soon learned that his knowledge was valuable to others. They appreciated him, and he began to appreciate himself.

But then a new difficulty appeared, as it often does, with many of us. Deep inside himself, Mr. Ranthrow was *very* self-appreciative. He cared so much for himself that he really did not want to expose the idealized image that he had set up in the inner recesses of his soul. He seldom committed himself because he never wanted to be in a situation where he would really make a mistake. So long as he kept quiet, he could always tell himself: "George, you really know what is best, but people would not understand if you told them." This was a topsy-turvy thought in the group. Here was a man who acted as though he despised himself. Actually, he was inwardly preening an image that was never revealed. It might never have come to anyone's attention if Mr. Wardhouse had not begun to express some deep doubts about himself during one session. No one seemed to really "get with" his fears and despair, and Mr. Wardhouse pushed people away by saying: "No one can really understand." He would shake his head and look at the floor. Finally the leader said: "George, how is it that you have nothing to contribute to Jack's dilemma?"

MR. RANTHROW: "Oh, I do feel for him. Yes, I do. I know just how miserable he must be. Yes. Yes."

LEADER: "Yes—what?"

MR. RANTHROW: (looking somewhat surprised) "I mean, he just feels deep down and all that. What did you have in mind?"

LEADER: "I had you in mind. You say that you have been through the same thing that he is going through, but you have offered no help. We have sat here for three-quarters of an hour and no one seems to get where Jack is. You say that you have been there. How come you don't help your brother?"

MR. RANTHROW: "Well, now, I want to be sure about

what I say. I can't really tell what another person is feeling."

LEADER: "Then suppose you tell what *you feel* about what he is saying."

MR. RANTHROW: "Well I'm not sure that I would be quite right in what I would say."

LEADER: "Oh? On several occasions I remember you telling us that you are quite sensitive to what other people are feeling. In fact, I believe that Jill congratulated you for that just last week."

MR. RANTHROW: "Yes, I guess that I am quite sensitive to what others are feeling. Yes, I do know something of what Jack is going through."

LEADER: "But you didn't tell him."

MR. RANTHROW: "Well, I'm not really accustomed or trained to speak up and tell people things like you are. We make some mistakes."

LEADER: "Wow! Now we are getting somewhere. You won't help your brother because you don't want to make a mistake. Ha. That's it!"

MR. RANTHROW: "Well, now it is easy for you to talk like that. You have training and lots of experience, but the rest of us don't have that."

MRS. TEDD: "You see, you sure are backtracking a lot today, George. I don't think you care anything about Jack at all."

MR. RANTHROW: "Well, now, I do not think that is quite fair. I do understand a good deal about what he is going through, but I don't think that I should be required to speak up and say everything that I think. I don't *really* know him. Wouldn't I look like a fool telling him some things that didn't really fit?"

MRS. TEDD: "What I hear you saying is that you are more concerned about being right than you are about sharing yourself with someone in need."

MR. RANTHROW: (looks at leader) "You understand, don't you?"

LEADER: "Well, maybe so. She has helped me to understand. You are more concerned about yourself than I had realized. I don't want to say that you have no concern for anybody else, but I guess I should say that you always want to have a *safe* concern. That is, you want to make sure that you don't make any mistakes when you speak. You don't seem to be so uncertain about yourself today, you seem to be certain about one thing, which is that you're going to be careful about your ideal picture of yourself as a person who doesn't make any mistakes."

What Are the Consequences?

Mr. Ranthrow was puzzled by the train of events. He frowned and protested. Several group members began to put the picture together (in the process, they seemed to forget the group member who had originally been the focus of their concern). Mr. Ranthrow was a man in dilemma. On the one hand, he wanted to show some concern for others because he was a sensitive person who could tell when they hurt, but at the same time, he would not risk himself. He must maintain the image of correctness at all times.

Mr. Ranthrow and the group were wrestling with the final question in decision-making: what are the consequences? All decisions have some consequences. A new one was now appearing to Mr. Ranthrow. When he did not share with his brother, people concluded that he had closed his heart. This was a consequence with which Mr. Ranthrow was most uncomfortable. He had hoped that by making no decision he would escape any judgments. Such is not the case; we are judged both by action and inaction. Decision and indecision have consequences.

The group was pushing Mr. Ranthrow to move toward good consequences, a show of concern for someone whom he understood. This risk in sharing would have far outweighed the bad consequences of a mistake in judgment about the fine points of another person's feeling. We can forgive much in those who intend the best for us. In fact, if Mr. Ranthrow could begin his speech with a statement that he did not understand everything, he would certainly have been well-received.

But Mr. Ranthrow was still uncertain. He was not quite sure of the ground on which he stood. This is understandable. We all hesitate in ambiguous circumstances (unless we are like Mrs. Ranthrow). We need to know what we can hold on to, what is secure when the way is uncertain. This is the question of dependency, to which we will now turn.

chapter 8
on whom can i depend?

If you get into a group, you have admitted some dependency on other people, but that very fact may have kept you out of a group for a long time. You may have felt that any admission of dependence upon others was an automatic loss of individuality. That's a popular assumption that has sometimes been fostered by scientific emphases. Dr. Gordon Allport of the psychology department of Harvard University wrote some years ago that many psychologists had sidestepped any serious study of the human desire for love and affection. They did not emphasize the importance of our tender relationships. Instead, much of the research and a great deal of popular writing was on discord, hostility, sexual conflict. In this flight from tenderness, psychologists missed the importance of the giving and receiving of affection.

Our basic need is to balance dependence with independence. This is difficult in the shifting culture of modern society. Some of the old guideposts are gone, and new ones have not yet appeared. In the meantime, the boss and other people require conformity, but are we giving in at the price of self-respect?

Finding the Guideposts

Each of us needs some principles for living. There must be some firm reference points in order to orient ourselves for the decisions of life. The framework for these decisions should be the teaching and approval of trusted persons and our inner development of conscience and wisdom. These reinforce each other. They enable us to resist the giving or accepting of attitudes that are inconsistent with our moral standards.

If we have developed peer guidelines over a period of years, a group discsusion will enable us to check our signposts against those which are being established by other people in our culture. Do they hear the same inner voice that urges us on? Do they explain their actions as we do? Are they uptight at the same time that we are, or do they seem relaxed and free about everything?

We compare landmarks by saying: "I see it this way," "Well, I see it differently." You may come out of one group session with a sense of relief that others are looking at life as you are, and then in the next session you may be amazed by the differences that appear. Whatever the issue, the group has helped to perform the same function from week to week. We are comparing positions with each other, checking our points of agreement and difference about life.

"Why, I never knew that you thought . . ." is one of the best rewards that we can hear during a session on guide-posts. People are really learning where others stand. Sometimes a group is very similar in values and outlook. Under these circumstances, we develop a deeper apprecia-tion of the individuality of those who are going in the same direction, but with their own outlook. Instead of seeing them as part of the crowd, we see them after our group sessions as persons who can be identified by taste, attitudes, opinions, and actions.

Other groups may show more diversity. The difference

may be in terms of moral and religious background or experience and age. I have found that a mixture of younger and older adults and teenagers can produce excellent satisfaction from everyone. The adolescents say that they can really be heard for the first time by adults. The middle-aged adults say that they now begin to understand what the adolescents are talking about. So long as mother and father, son and daughter are not in the same group, these results are possible. (In family counseling an entire family is together. This is not the same as our present subject, group experience.)

Again and again, people come out of these varied groups to say: "I needed to learn that from those people." The adult has learned from the youngster, the adolescent from the parental figure, the man from the woman, the woman from the man. Some people may say that this learning is already available to them in their life experiences. Maybe so, but our culture is shifting too fast for that kind of certainty. We need to lean some on each other to learn what is going on in modern life.

The need for learning is most acute for those who are cut off from previous life experiences in which people really talked about themselves. No guidelines were given because no one was very concerned to teach other members of the family or community. This deficiency has often been noted in delinquent adults and adolescents. One answer is a group technique that is called rational emotive therapy.

The assumption of rational emotive therapy is that many people do not understand or feel the basic meaning of the great words of life. Love, honesty, bravery, charity, beauty are just "words." In a group setting, the leader asks people to describe an example of this word in their own life experience. Some of the members have nothing to contribute, and others give very distorted answers. The work of the leader is first to tell what the word means and then to help his group experience that meaning. Some member may give an example that is close to the meaning that is commonly accepted by society. If so, there is more discussion of how we can develop that understanding or what has kept us from it.

Men and women who have had a hard time with life and who are paying for their mistakes are often blocked from any awareness of tender emotion. They do not really know how to admit their dependency upon others, for their dependent needs have never been met in a healthy way. Love, affection, forgiveness, understanding are wonderful words that have been denied in their lives. It is only over a period of weeks or months that they can painfully admit their need for this basic nurture in life. When they can admit their need for others, the group begins to grow as a living family.

This family meaning of a group is also found in Synanons and other associations of "dope fiends." This is the name that the members give to each other and to themselves. The group strives for self-awareness, confession, honesty, awareness of the needs of others. A substitute family is created. In some instances, a person has been so deprived from childhood that he cannot live outside of this substitute group. He may work during the day, but he returns to his new family at night.

Less deprived people will not need a permanent home, but they may need some brief companionship in a new and isolating environment. The popularity of group experiences, marathons, and other growth encounters in large cities may be accounted for in part by the depersonal atmosphere of a metropolis. People really do not know each other, and they cannot find a place where anyone would care if they were there or not. Group therapy and its derivatives are one means of sharing as a human being with someone else. The encounter group may be very much like the Saturday supper of a large family, but that family has left the home place. A substitute is needed until new moorings can be established.

Temporary Sustenance

The need for community may be raised by a move to a large city or the isolating effects of a competitive suburban surrounding. But there are many other circumstances under which we need to be sustained by a group for a short period of time. Group therapy began in Boston with the recognized need for tubercular patients to come together for a discussion of their problems and a development of cohesion through the long period of convalescence. This convalescent-type group has continued in physical medicine, sometimes to sustain people who are chronically ill and more often to rehabilitate those who need a sense of belonging to move back into health. The group actually forms a cheering section for persons who are making a painful and slow adjustment.

Both by teaching and example, a temporary handicap may be overcome. Persons who have suffered from the same illness may come back into a group after they have "made it" in the community. I have seen the rapt attention of soldiers who have lost a limb as they watched a lecturer who was wearing an artificial hand. He didn't talk about his "handicap" until after the lecture. Then he brought the men into a group to ask if they would like to do what he was doing and how they felt right now about themselves. As they begin to open up their frustrations and hopes, he shared his own resolute journey from the shock of loss on the battlefield to a sense of security in a new business.

The loss may be more emotional than physical in some cases. Widows and widowers are certainly going to ask: "Who can I appropriately depend upon?" In our fast-moving society, there may be no reliable person to lean on over a period of time. I believe that this is one reason for admissions to a mental hospital. Most of the people who come into the hospital have had some major grief experience within the past year. Sometimes it is the loss of a loved one, sometimes it is a severe business reverse or moral failure. The psychological collapse of the individual did not "just happen." It was the result of severe deprivation. A needed support in life was removed, and there was nothing to take its place.

As mental health has moved into the community, more attention has been given to the need for short-term sustaining groups. In the summer of 1972, Harvard University sponsored a seminar to train widows as group leaders for bereaved persons. In the ghettos of large cities, these women who had successfully moved through grief to a new grasp of life were the rallying points for other persons who were cut off and desperately alone. There are some times when we really need to lean upon others. If the family and close friends are not at hand, or do not understand, then a special group may meet our natural needs.

Protection for Life

Will our dependency needs be greater if we suffer some handicap for life? A person who is physically incapacitated or who is mentally retarded may seem to be a very special case. We often think that these persons will be full of self-pity, or we pity them. We may have met some who were very aggressive and irritable or overly dependent and grasping.

If you do suffer from some handicap or find this in your family, you may resent these stereotypes. You know that it is the self-concept of the handicapped person that really determines character and performance. This is why some special interest groups are most valuable to persons who need a healthy outlook on their physical limitations. Dr. Carney Landis found that physically handicapped women did admit a good deal of frustration when they thought about their childhood. There were many activities in which they could not participate. But, as adults, these women did not talk a great deal about themselves. They were somewhat restricted in their interest towards other people, but they were not turned in upon themselves. There was no gross amount of frustration, annoyance, or hopelessness. Instead, they exhibited a normal amount of independence in all areas except those affected by their physical disability.

We can see the importance of a group for handicapped children. They can hardly wait for the bus to take them in the morning to kindergarten and in later years, to a sheltered workshop. Here they find people who are like them, or who understand these special needs of their livelihood. An adaptation has been made to a limitation in life. This does not distort living, it only causes a readjustment.

The Yes-sayers

Our most difficult psychological problem is with the overly-adjusted individual. This is the person who is handicapped by a continual tendency to say "yes."

Are you a yes-sayer? You will probably check "yes" by each of the following statements:

I don't like to work on a problem unless there is a possibility of coming out with a clear-cut and unambiguous answer.

Once I have made up my mind, I seldom change it.

It is all right to get around the law if you don't actually break it.

Most people are honest, chiefly through fear of being caught.

When I meet a stranger I often think that he is better than I am.

Sometimes I am sure that other people can tell what I am thinking.

I wish that I could get over worrying about things I have said that may have injured other peoples feelings.

I commonly wonder what hidden reason another person may have for doing something nice for me.

People pretend to care more about one another than they really do. These statements were developed and tested by Richard Crutchfield and reported in "Conformity and Character," *The American Psychologist* 10 (1955), p. 195.

Are these your statements? If so, a group is a good place to look at some of the problems that this way of thinking will cause in your life. If you will commit the necessary time and openness to the discussion, some of the deadly sins of dependency will be met: self-contempt, sloth, envy, jealousy, self-deception, dogmatism.

Charlie was a yes-sayer who saw some of these problems. In a young adult group, he was always concerned about his image. He tried to look interested without looking so interested that someone would ask him what he was thinking. He nodded approval to people who were contradicting each other. When someone would ask him why he agreed with opposite opinions, he would say that he just wanted to be understanding.

From week to week, Charlie would try to think of something to say in the group seminar that would contribute to the discussion without drawing attention to himself. He and his wife were most distressed. They often talked of his problem. How could he assert himself without making others angry with him? When he tried so hard to do what was right, why was he not recognized and approved?

Gradually Charlie became aware of more uncomfortable feelings. He was actually envious of others who won approval. He was continually blaming himself for not having their abilities. He did not like this combination of self-contempt and jealousy.

In addition to the group experience, Charlie was receiving some individual supervision for his work as a counselor. Here he learned that he was of real benefit to certain types of clients. Those who were shy and dependent were always the first to seek him out in the clinic. He had a respect for these people that won their affection. They knew that he would not hurt them. At the same time, his earnest desire to be of help was apparent. They knew that he would assist them, even though he would be slow. He was affirmed by his supervisor for this ability.

Charlie was never able to affirm himself with his peers in the group. Each week, he would think about it, but then decide that it would be too boastful for him to proclaim how he was helping clients that others would disregard. In the individual sessions he could admit that his own need to depend on other people was a good reason for his ability to understand the shy and insecure clients who clung to him. He needed them as they needed him. At least he understood what was happening in him and had some control over the relationships.

A year after the completion of counselor training Charlie was appointed director of a small town mental health clinic. When I visited in the area, I heard him praised for dependability, sincerity, concern for other people. He did not speak up much in meetings, but that did not seem to matter. He "got along" with those in power because he was not self-assertive. They trusted him to do his job well and left him to make his own decisions about the clinic. As we talked over these observations, he laughed and said: "You and the others gave me a hard time because I would not speak up in the seminar. I know what you were trying to do. I appreciate it. But here, it works to my advantage; since I have an education and still don't say much, people think that I am very wise. I heard that one of the board members said he was glad that they had a young man who knew his business—and his place."

Absolute and Relative Dependence

A group can meet many of our dependent needs, but not all of them. This is a difficult lesson for some people to learn. You may have known someone who has been in a group that has meant much for him or her. The person talks in the highest terms of the group experience. It seems that all the needs of an individual are met through those sessions.

If your friend feels this way for a few weeks and then begins to broaden his contacts and share more of himself with other people, he has done well. But if he insists that this group is his absolute source of security and that all other relationships are as nothing when compared to it, then he is asking for more than any group can bear.

There will be times when any one of us are almost completely dependent upon the help of others. It may be in the crisis of illness, bereavement, or the slow climb toward convalescence. Sometimes we learn a great deal during particular sessions of a group and realize how much we are at the mercy of others to learn vital lessons about ourselves.

But most of us will move through these periods of relative dependence to a new level of independence. We will have learned something from the group that will help us in life outside that relationship.

Instead of an absolute dependence, the group should give us a sense of creativity in the midst of the insecurities of modern life. In the group, we can become more aware of our limitations, we can give up some of our defenses against the recognition that we are not always right and secure. We can seriously consider how dependent we are at times upon others.

Most essentially, we can recognize the anchors of life. What do we live for? Toward what goals are we striving?

Whom do we need to help us in this struggle? Whom can we help along the way?

These are questions that give us security in the midst of uncertainty. They provide firm ground from which we can launch out into some new territory. There will be times when we must return to some kind of group for reaffirmation and nurture, but this does not have to become a chronic habit. We learn in a protected environment now so that we can be of better service to others in the tumults of daily life.

The group is only an oasis. It is a place to refresh ourselves, reorient our attitudes toward others, restore self-awareness and reeducate us in interpersonal relations. We still have to confront life, make commitments, endure compromises with people who did not go to a session on sensitivity awareness, no matter how much we may think that they need what we have experienced. We need to learn Lucy's second lesson for Charlie Brown.

CHARLIE BROWN: My trouble is I never know if I'm doing the right thing. I need to have someone around who can tell me when I am doing the right thing.

LUCY: O.K.—You're doing the right thing—That will be five cents please. (Charlie Brown walks away. In a few minutes he returns.)

LUCY: Back already? What happened?

CHARLIE BROWN: I was wrong—it didn't help—you need more in life than just having someone around to tell you when you are doing the right thing.

LUCY: Now you've *really* learned something. That will be another five cents please! ("Peanuts" by Schulz in the *Atlanta Constitution,* Sunday, June 10, 1973.)

reading guide for group experience

(prepared with the assistance of Jacob Christ, M.D., chairman, Atlanta Group Psychotherapy Association)

Sharing Groups

The general subject of intimate conversations between small groups of normal persons in a church fellowship has been described by Robert C. Leslie in *Sharing Groups in the Church* (Abingdon Press, 1971). The author distinguishes sharing groups from psychotherapy groups and encourages the former in church fellowships. Case studies and examples are included. Related works are: Clyde Reid, *Groups Alive—Church Alive* (Harper & Row, 1969); Robert Raines, *New Life* in the Church (Harper & Row, 1961); John Casteel, editor, *Spiritual Renewal Through Personal Groups* (Association Press, 1957); and *The Creative Role of Interpersonal Groups in the Church Today* (Association Press, 1968).

Sensitivity and Encounter Groups

A comprehensive presentation of interpersonal encounters has been provided by Martin Lakin through *Interpersonal Encounter: Theory and Practice in Sensitivity Training* (McGraw Hill Book Co., 1972). The author describes the rationale for training, including examples of how people feel as participants in group training. Problems and issues in encounter groups are then presented. A final section discusses some current applications of encounter groups.

Some of the more well-known and controversial encounter groups are presented by articles in the December, 1967, issue of *Psychology Today.* Michael Murphy describes the Esalen experience. Carl Rogers ranges in his discussion from the value of the National Training Laboratories to Esalen and other workshops.

A number of cassette tapes have been developed to instruct and encourage group encounters, such as "Encountertapes," a Western Behavioral Sciences Institute production by Bell and Howell and the "Serendipity" series by Creative Resources of Waco, Texas.

Several evaluations of sensitivity and group therapy meetings have been prepared. The most basic is by Irvin Yalom, Morgan Lieberman, and Matthew Miles. A short summary may be found in the March, 1973, issue of *Psychology Today.* A more extensive report is in their 1973 book *Encounter Groups: First Results* (Basic Books). An evaluation of the "New Groups" is given by Irvin Yalom in a chapter of

The Theory and Practice of Gro 1970).

An evaluation of and recom training in educational and Sensitivity Training," an artic 15, 1969, issue of *Saturday*

A useful warning abou Shostrom, "Group Thera *Today*, May, 1969. He presen therapy.

(1) Never respond to a newspaper ad.
(2) Never participate in a group of fewer than six me
(3) Never join an encounter group on impulse.
(4) Never participate in a group encounter with close associates.
(5) Never be overly impressed by beautiful or otherwise class signal surroundings or participants.
(6) Never stay with a group that has a behavioral ax to grind.
(7) Never participate in a group that lacks formal connection with a professional on whom you can check.

Favorable evaluations of a marathon group under sponsorship of a church-related human potential organization may be found in Gerald and Elisabeth Jud's *Training in the Art of Loving* (United Church Press, 1972).

Group Therapy

The most comprehensive and readable text is *Theory and Practice of Group Psychotherapy* by Irvin Yalom (Basic Books, 1970). It is an excellent teaching textbook.

A volume richly endowed with examples is *Psychotherapy Through The Group Process* by Dorothy Whitaker and Morton Lieberman (Atheron Press, 1964). This is a comprehensive statement on group psychotherapy based on the assumption that understanding of the problem solving process in a group is the essential ingredient in solving our emotional problems.

Up to date and relevant papers on both group and family therapy have been edited by Clifford Sager and Helen Kaplan, *Progress in Group and Family Therapy*.

Succinct formulations of group work are contained in Paul Hare's *Handbook of Small Group Research*. The first chapter on elements of social interaction is especially valuable.

The problem of social pressure upon an individual is examined by Solomon Asch in a chapter of *Group Psychotherapy and Group Function* (Basic Books 1963) edited by Berger and Rosenbaum.